Dream & Desire

Coloring Book Therapy

Evolution Vol 3

Andrea Wood Schmitz

Published by Inkovator Publishing Company in 2015
First Edition, First Printing

Illustrations and Design © 2015 Andrea Wood Schmitz
http://inkovator.com

copyright@inkovator.com

ISBN-13: 978-1518883026

ISBN-10: 1518883028

Dedication

And now these three remain: Faith, hope and love. But the greatest of these is love.

1 Corinthians 13:13

No matter how you dice it, we've all been born into a family. Not all look alike, but it's a simple fact: no one willed himself or herself into existence.

Dream and Desire is volume 3 in the Evolution series, Coloring Book Therapy. And it is born out of love and as a family project in the summer of 2015.

This volume is dedicated to two people, to Yael, who is so young that she remembers neither of her grandmas. And to my mother, who lives across the Atlantic ocean, a world away, and who's having great health challenges at this point in time.

It's highly likely that by the time you read these lines, my mother has passed on. And that is why this book exists: to bridge the generations even when we cannot spend time together.

Here I take life lessons I learned from my mom and share them with my 6 year old in a fun, whimsical manner. May you enjoy coloring this as much as we did compiling the pages that follow!

Use this page as your
Color Test Page
For your markers, pencils and crayons

Place a piece of paper UNDERNEATH this page to test if your markers bleed through!

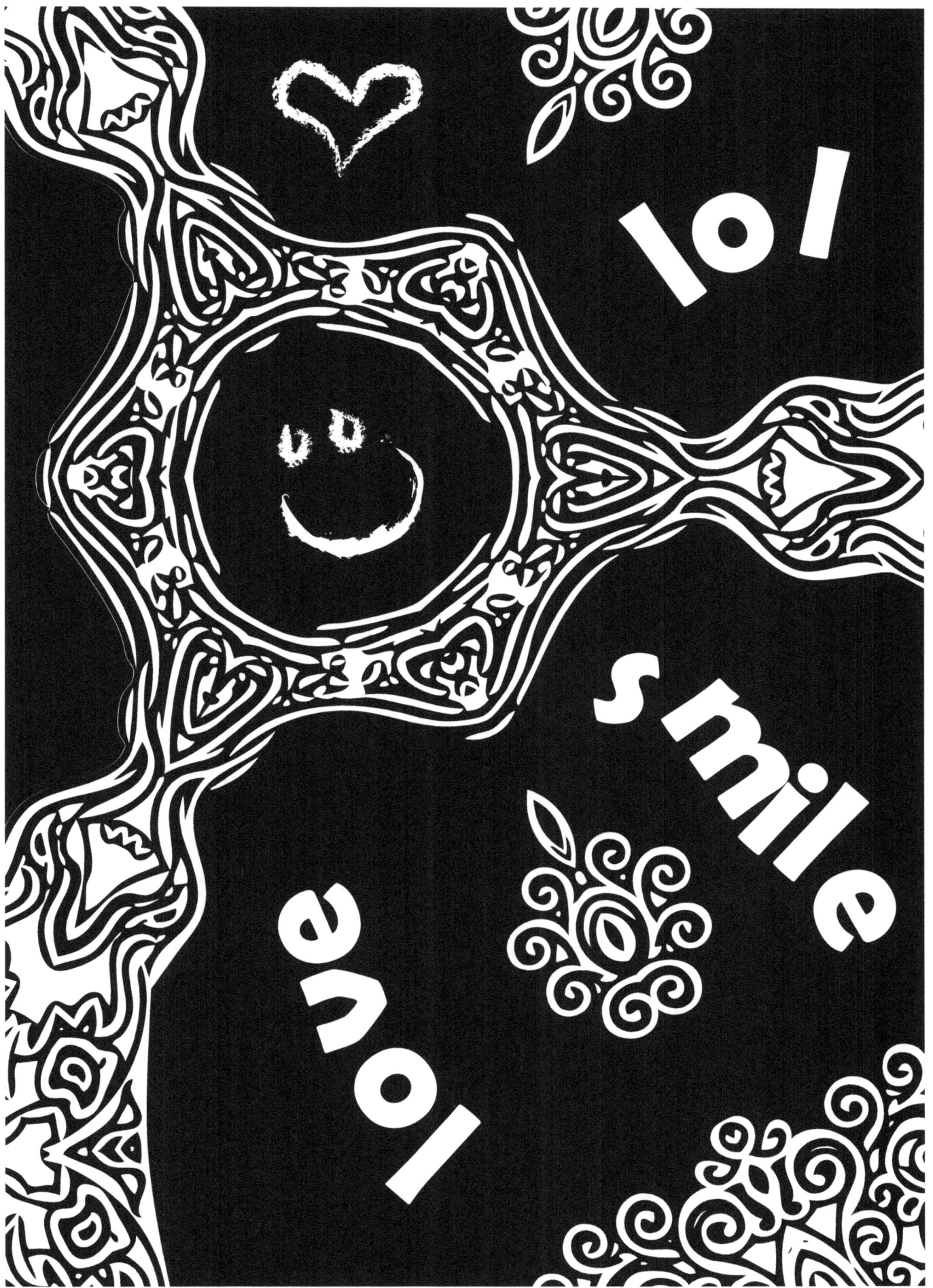

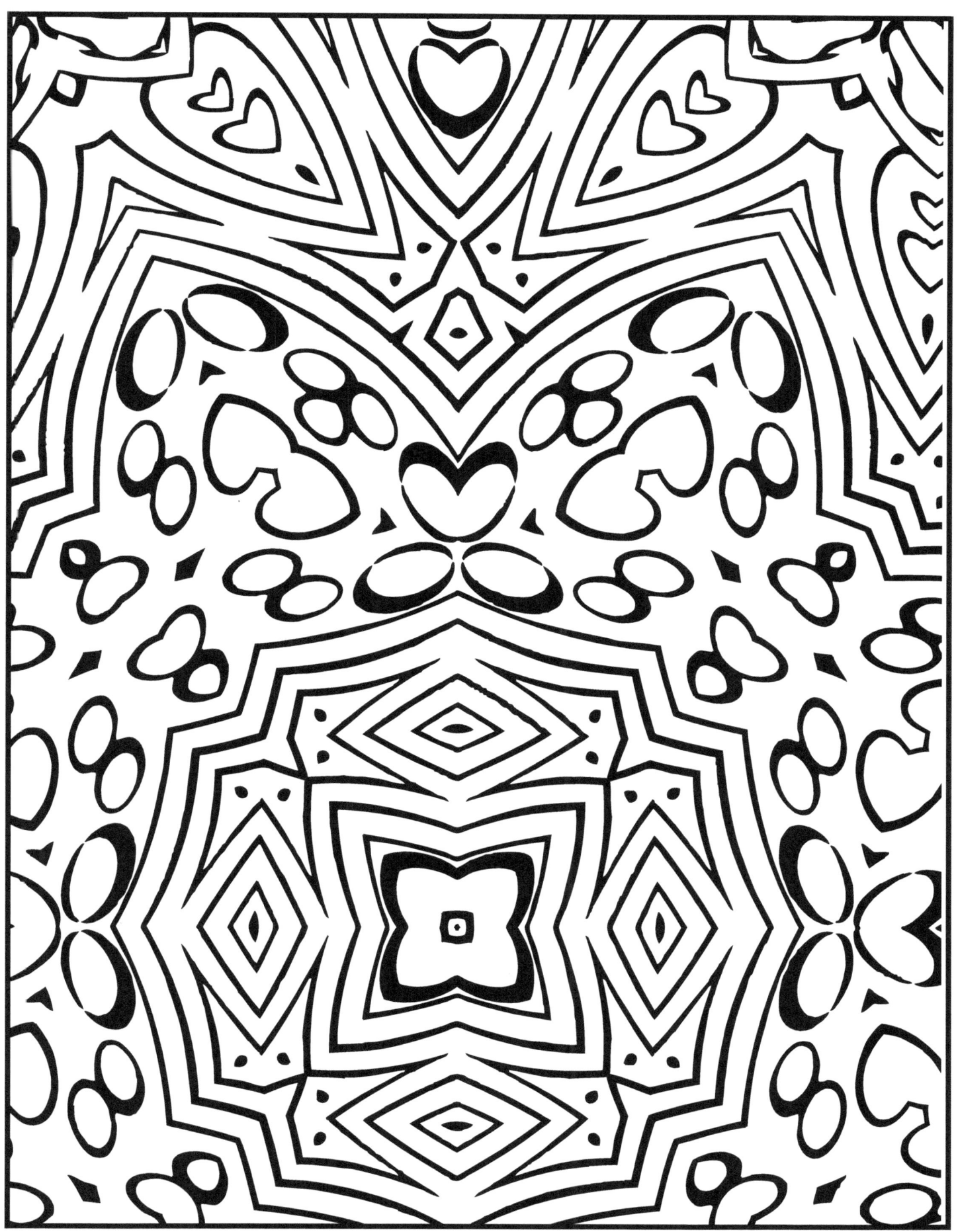

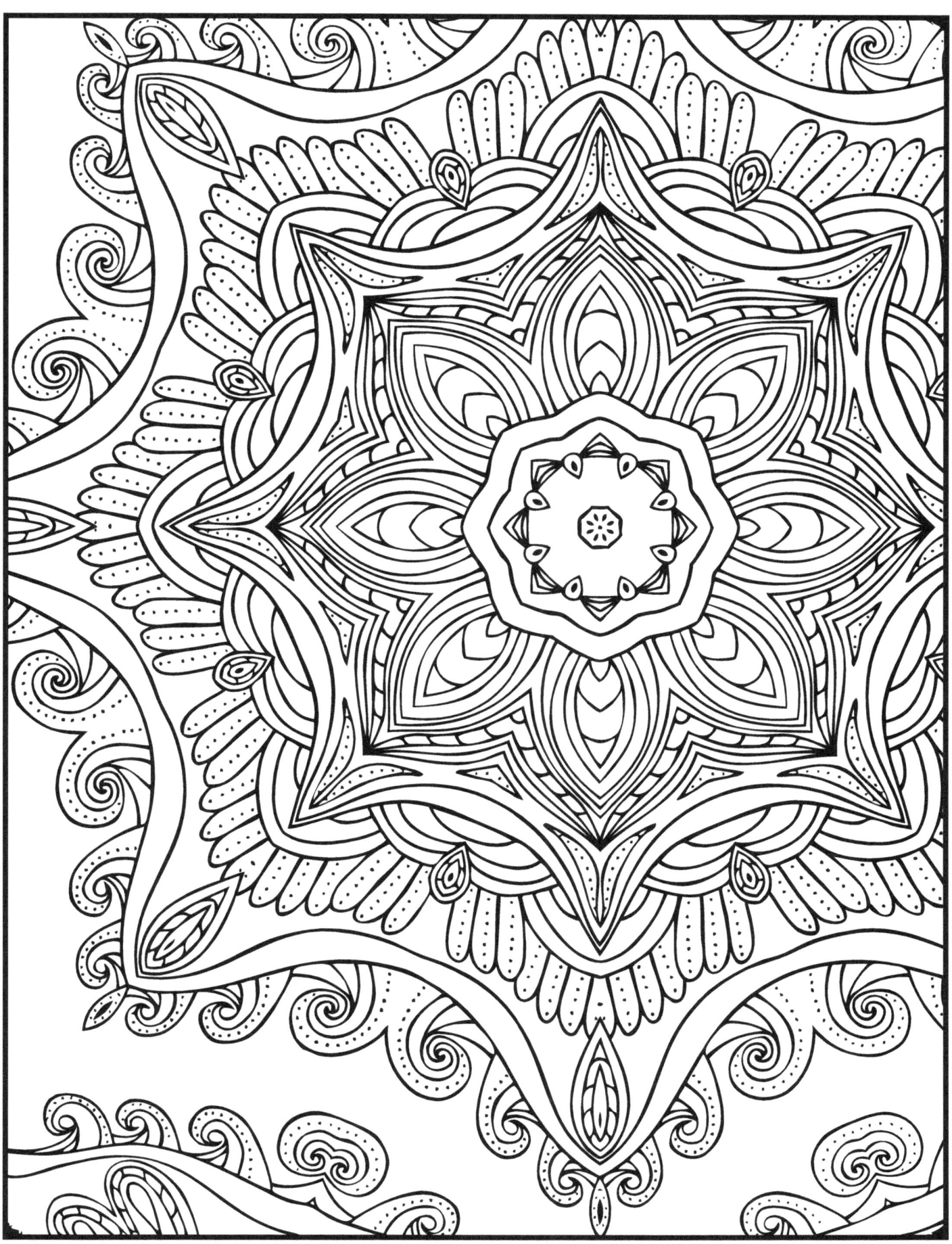

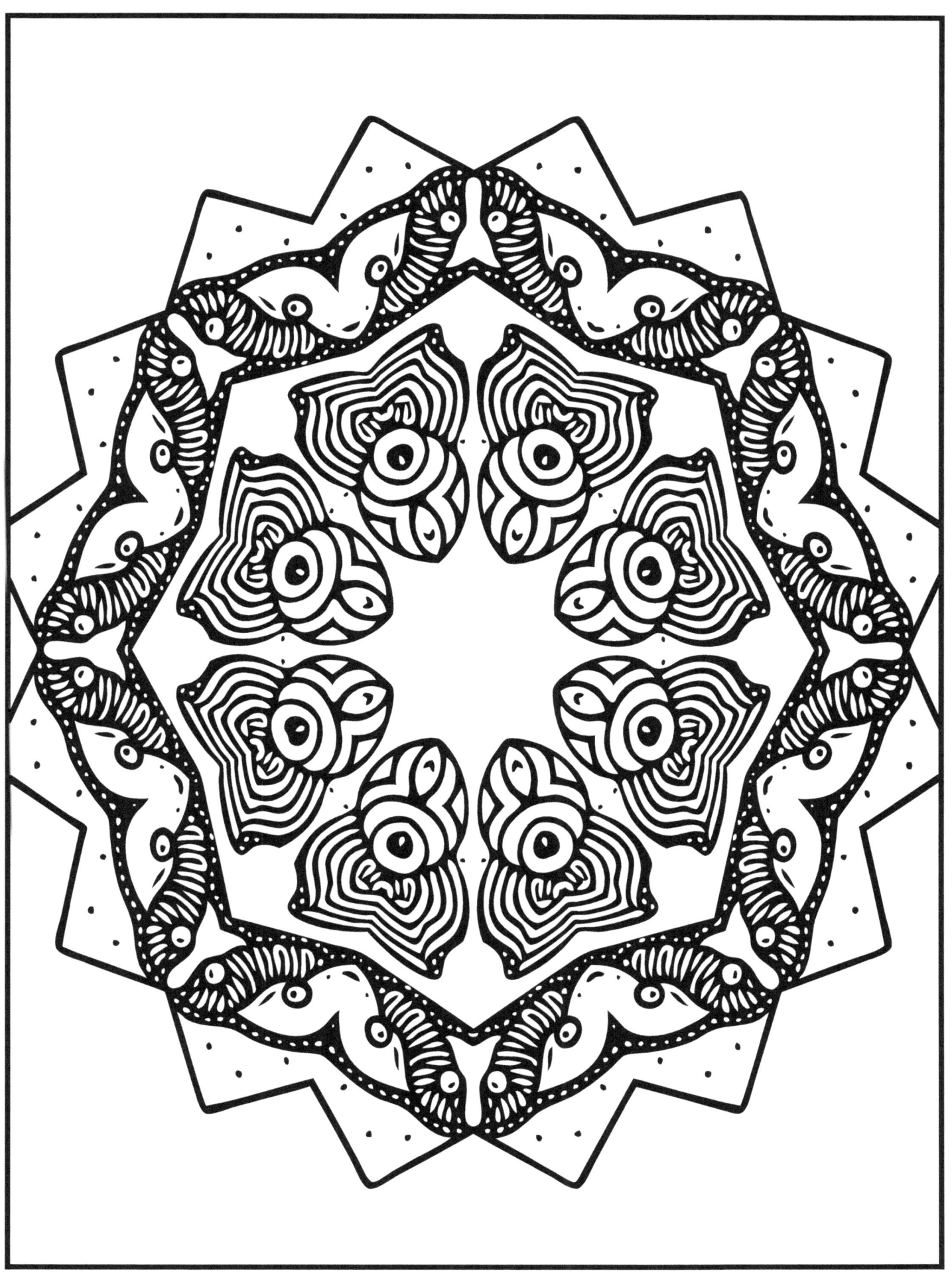

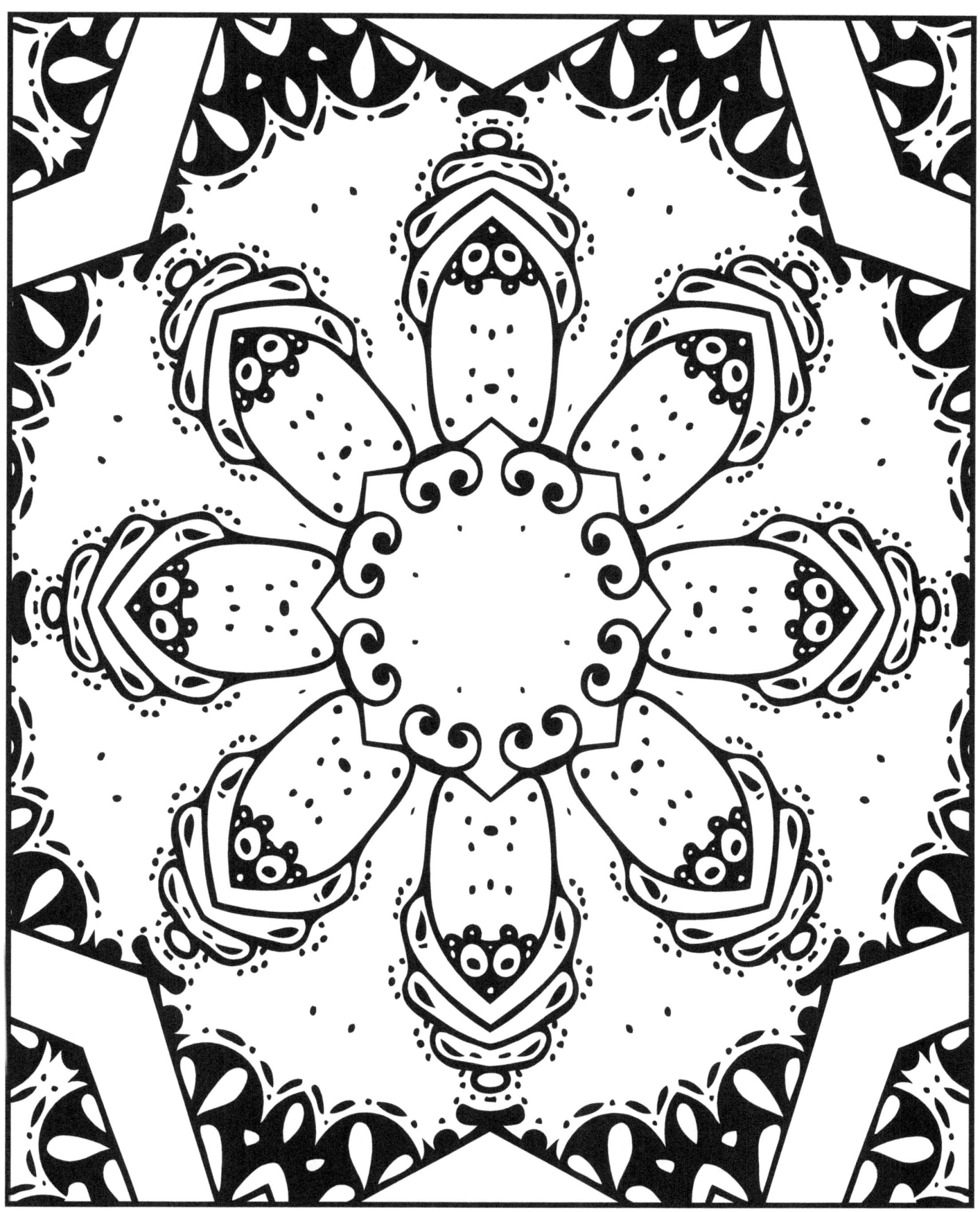

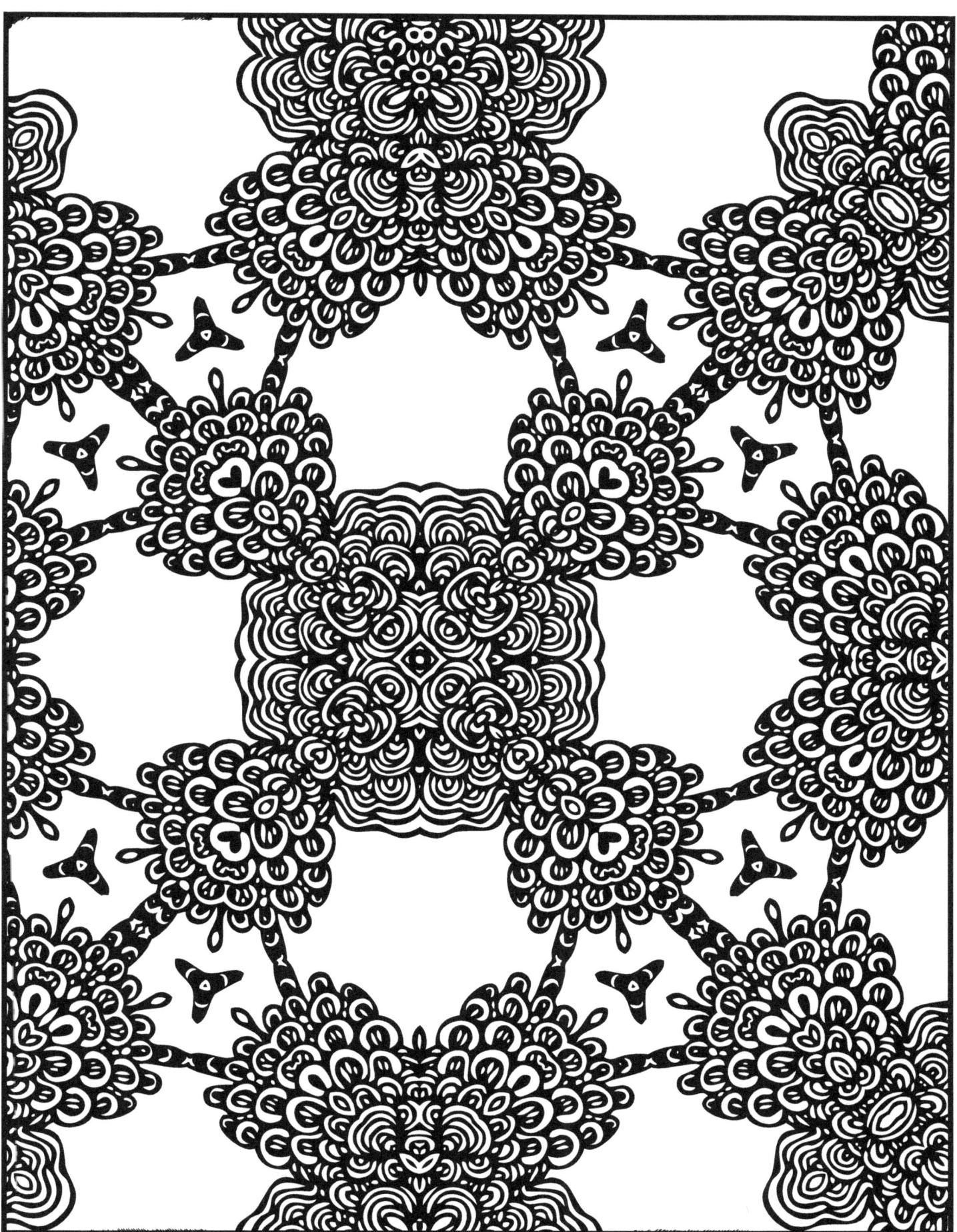

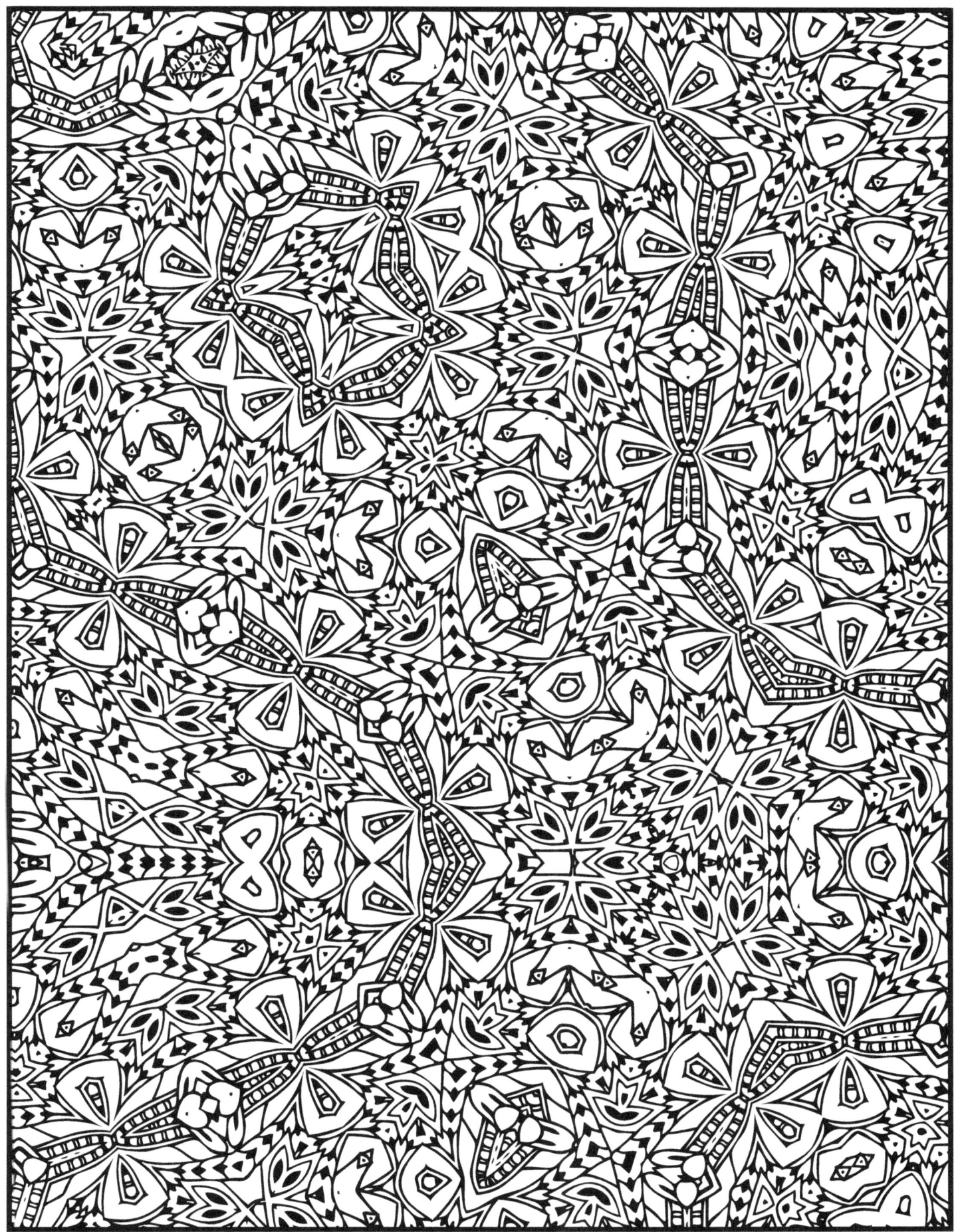

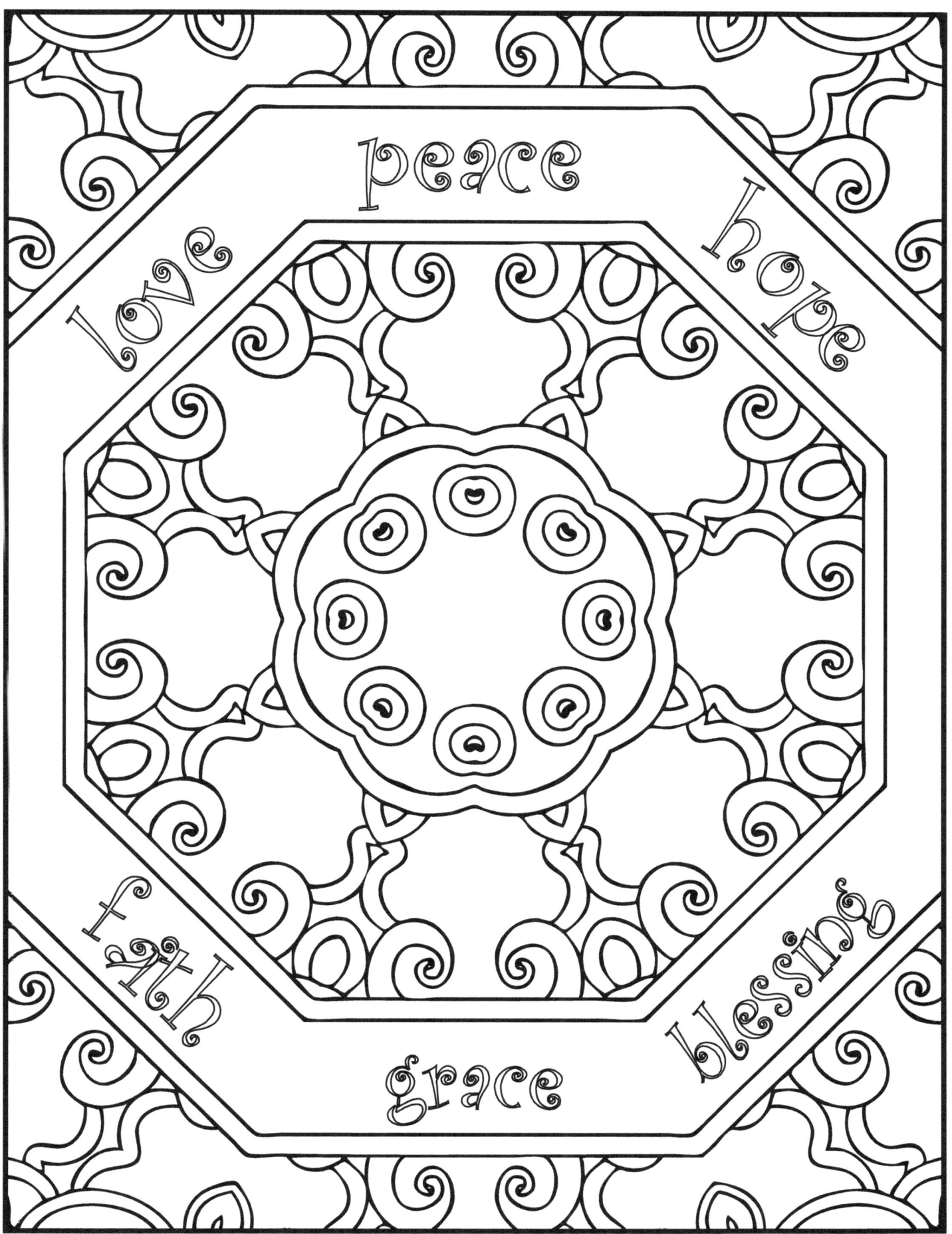

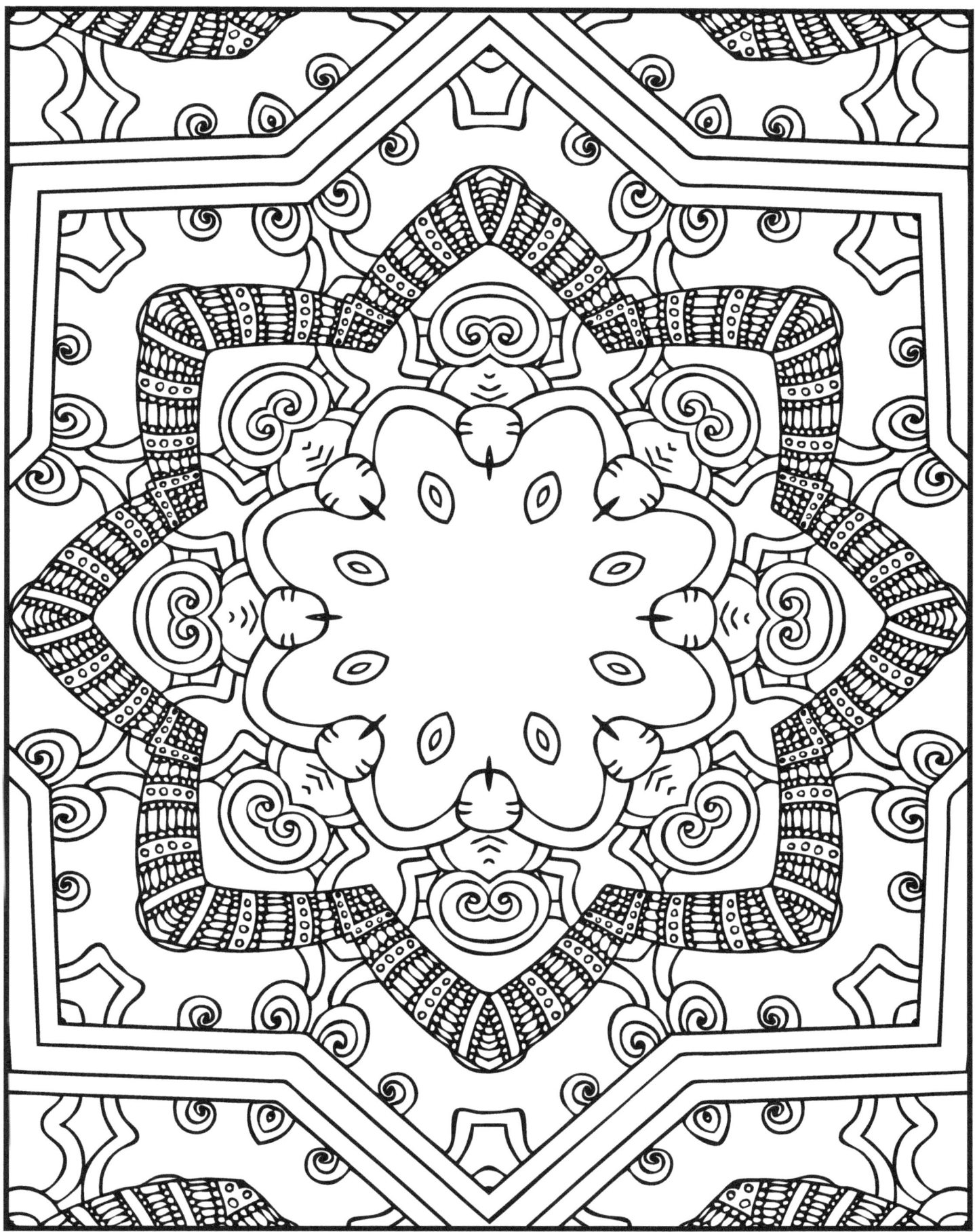

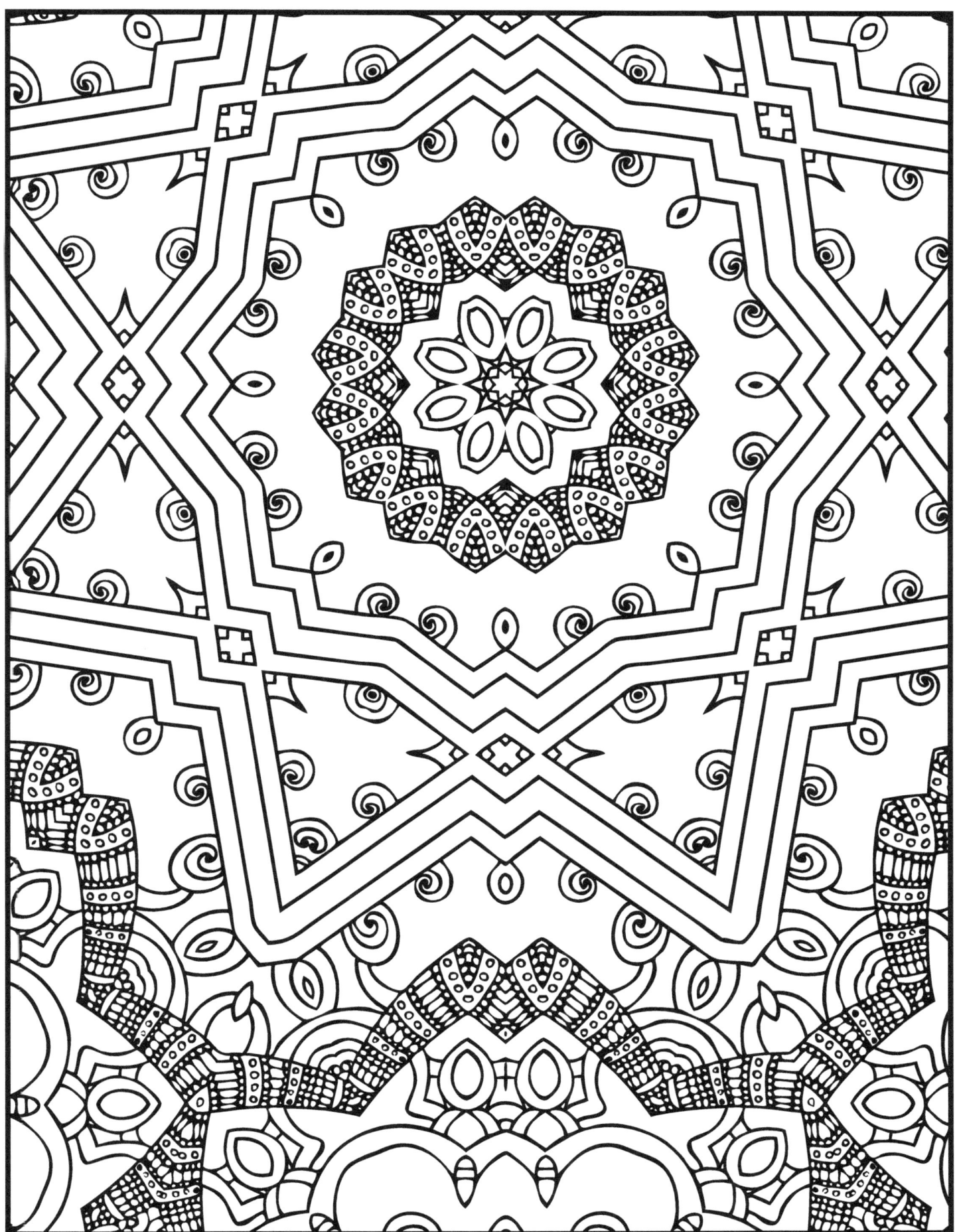

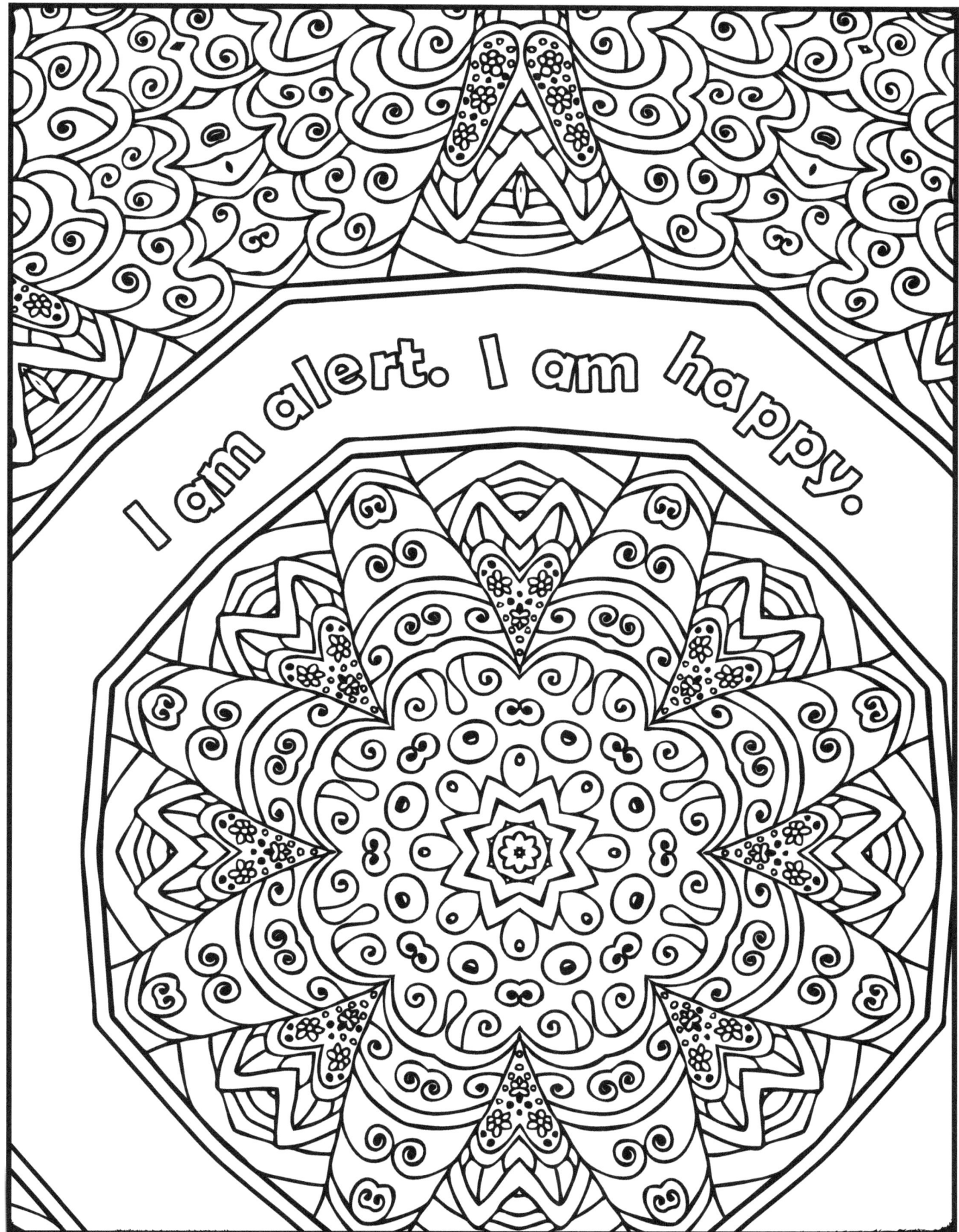

I love the flowers!

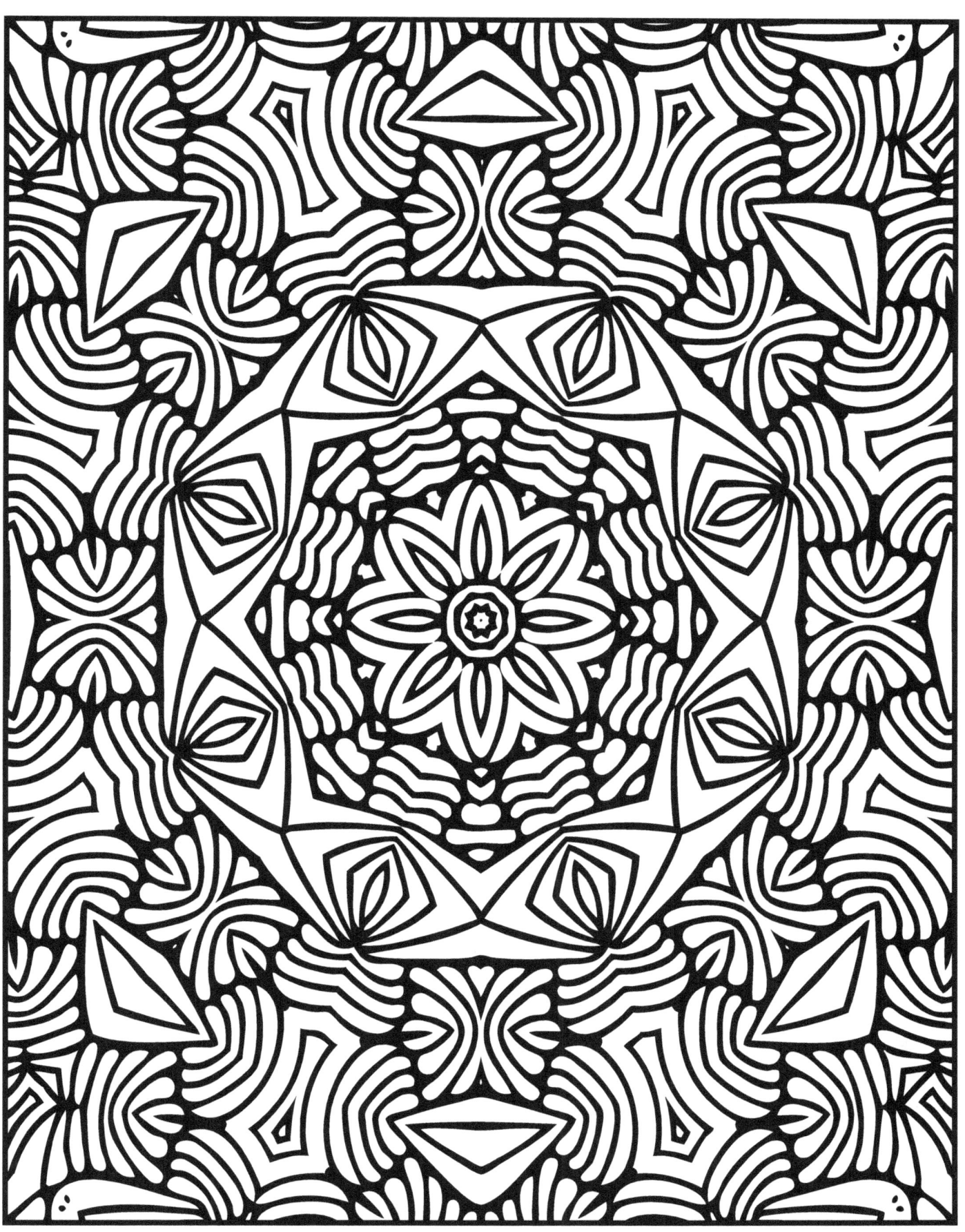

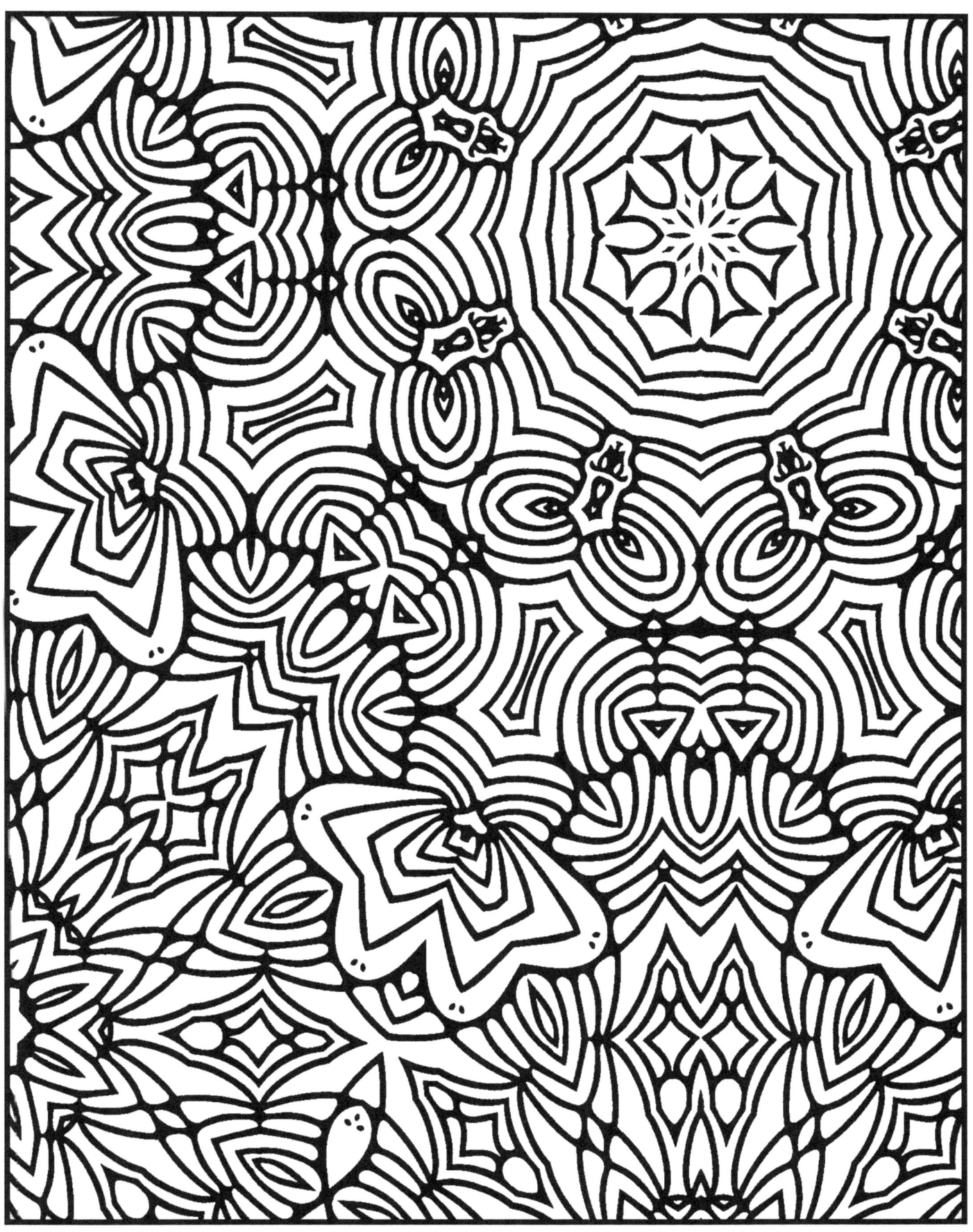

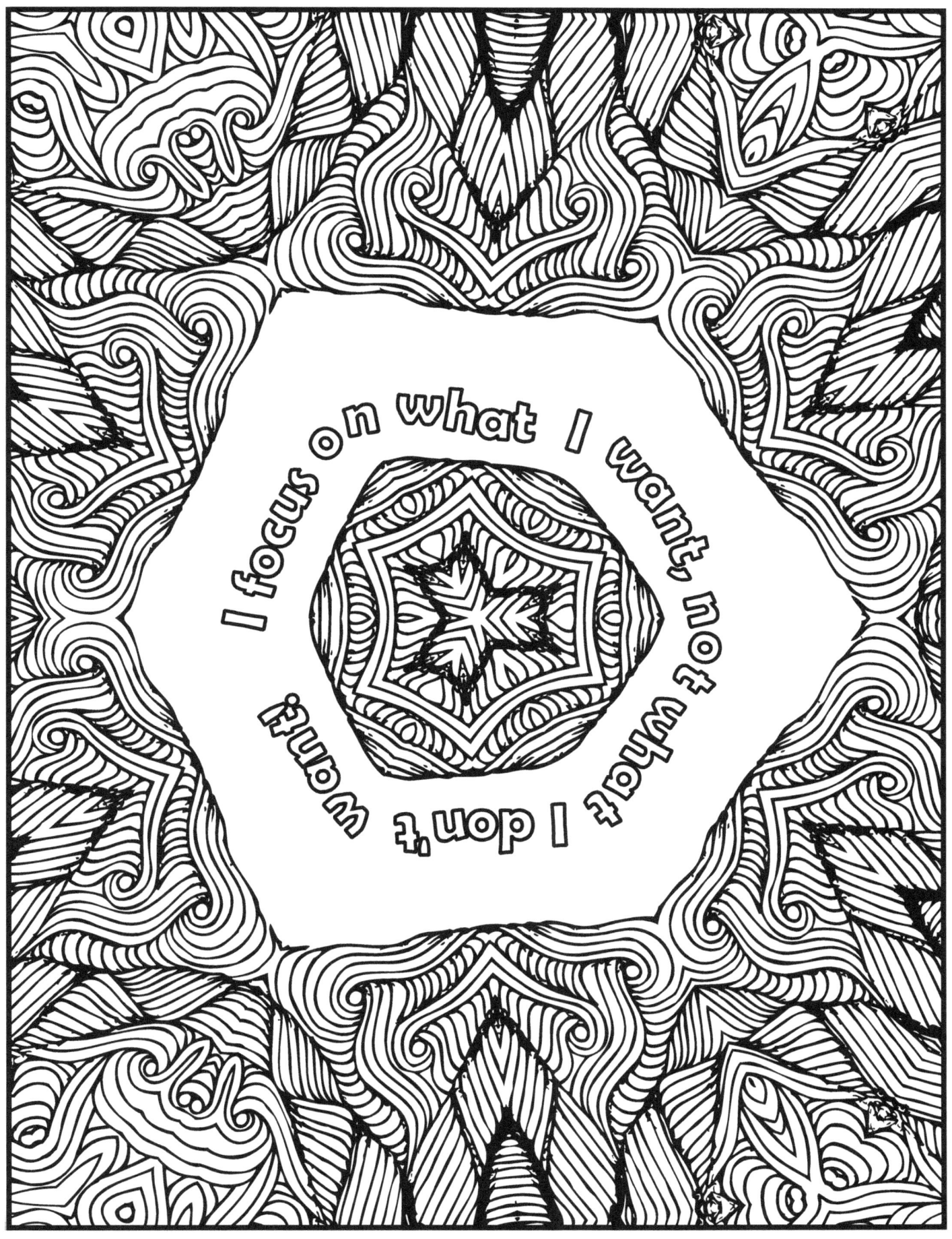

I focus on what I want, not what I don't want!

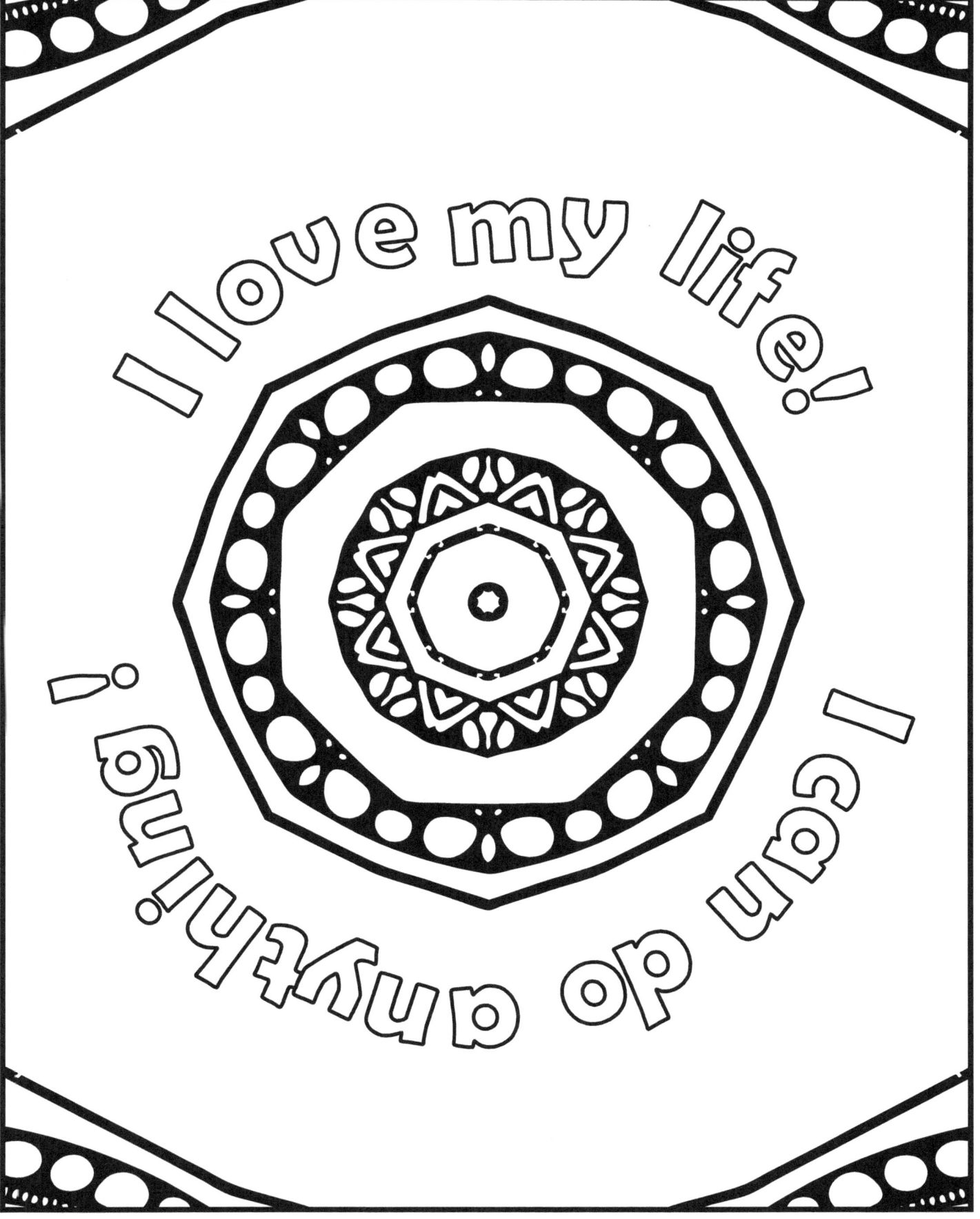

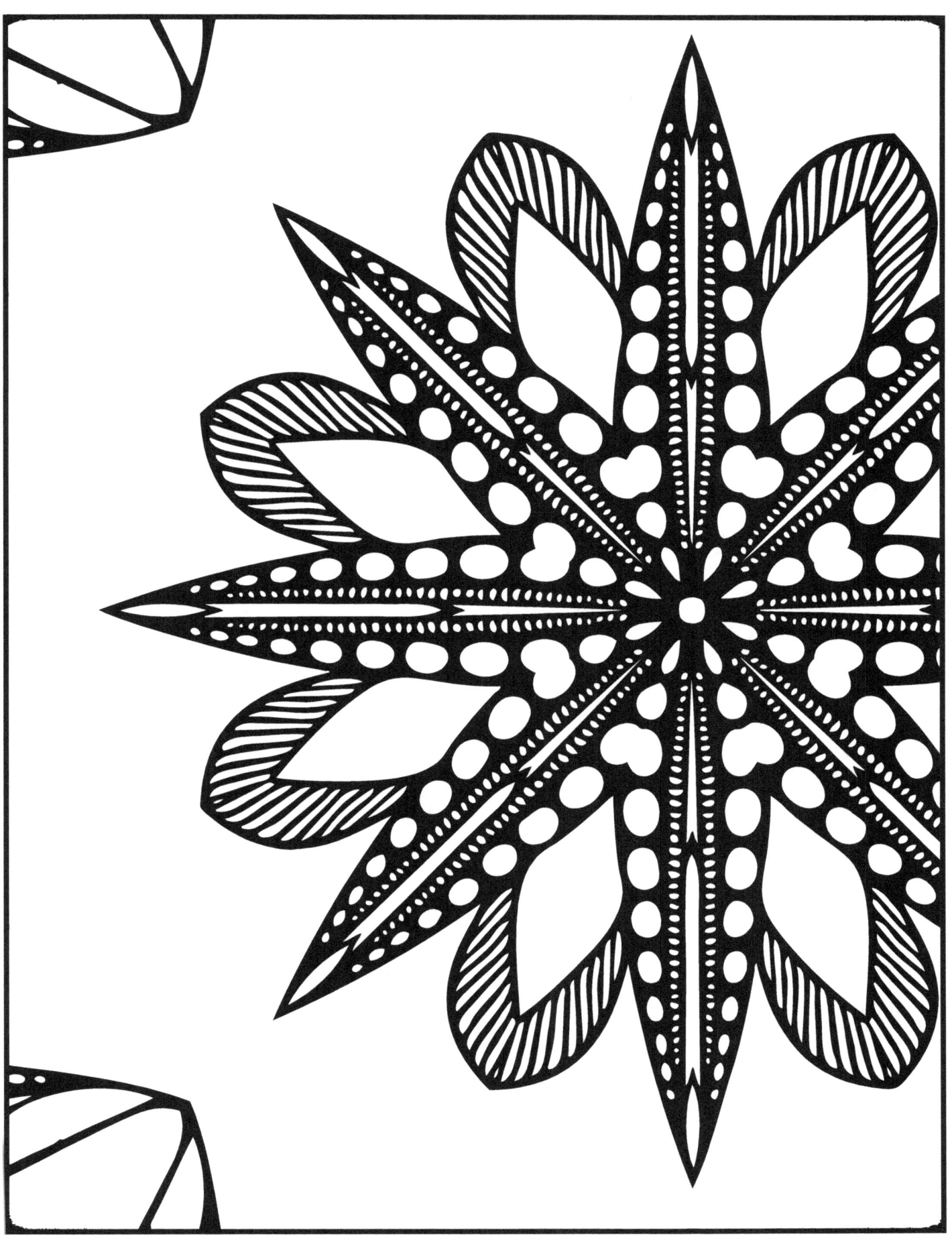

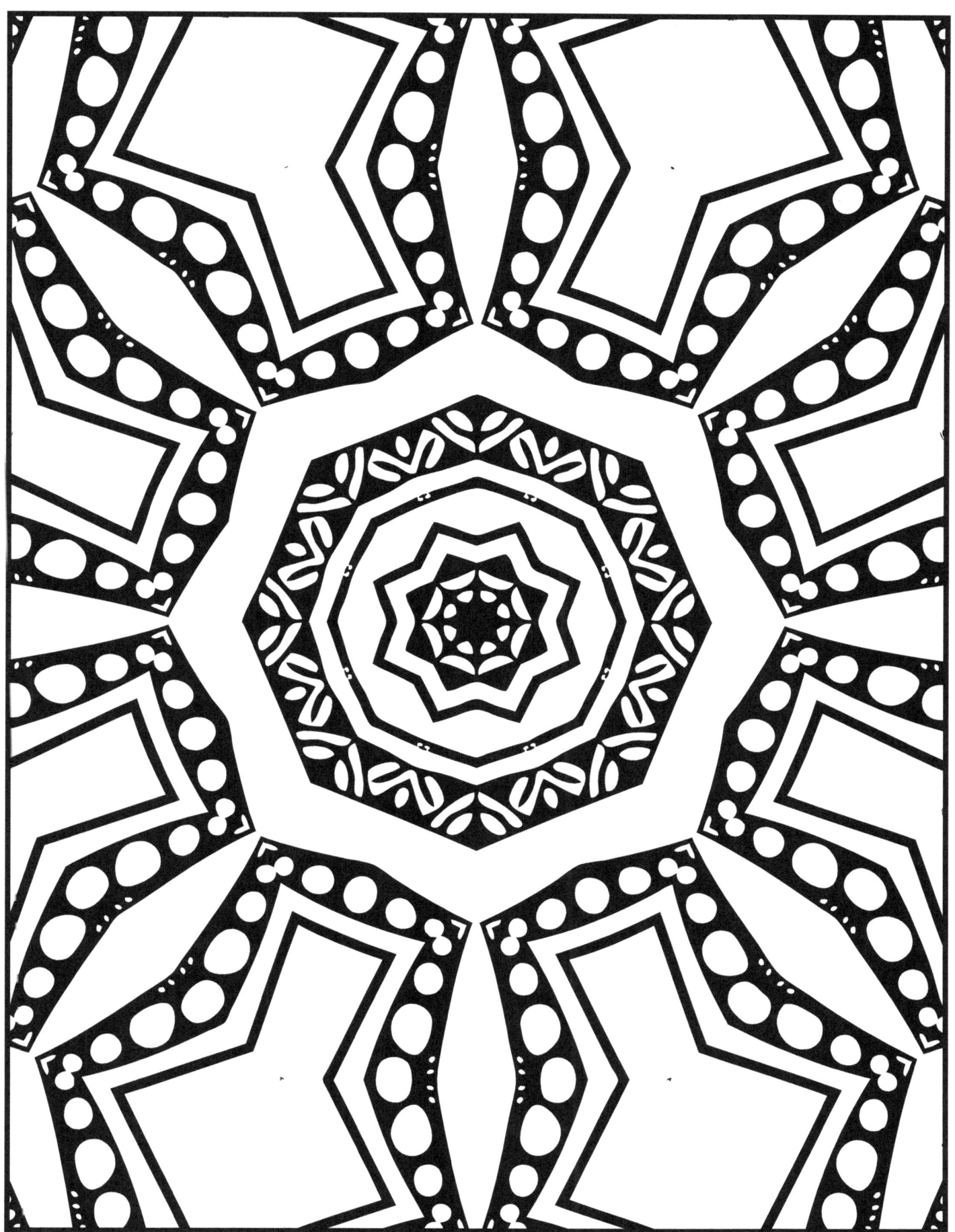

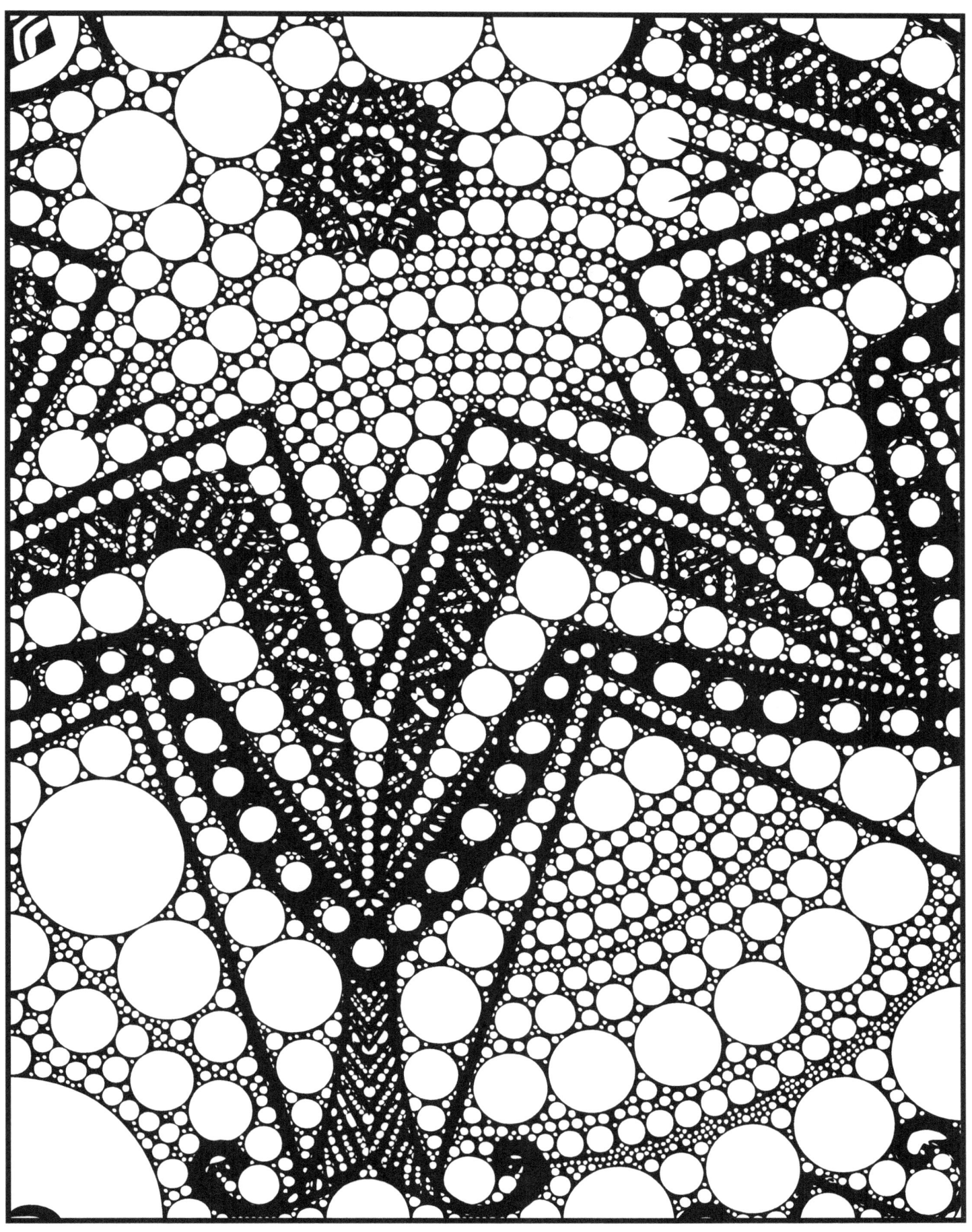

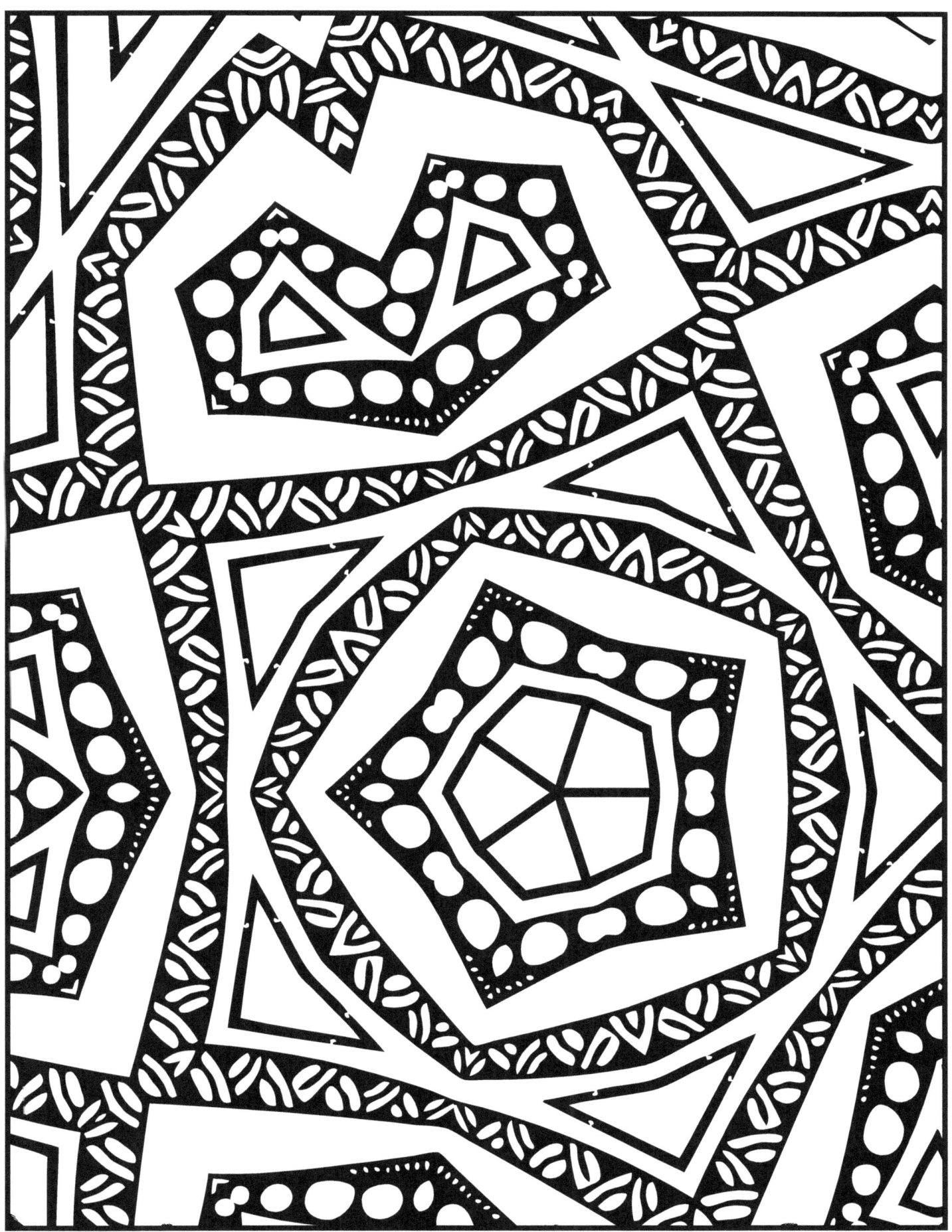

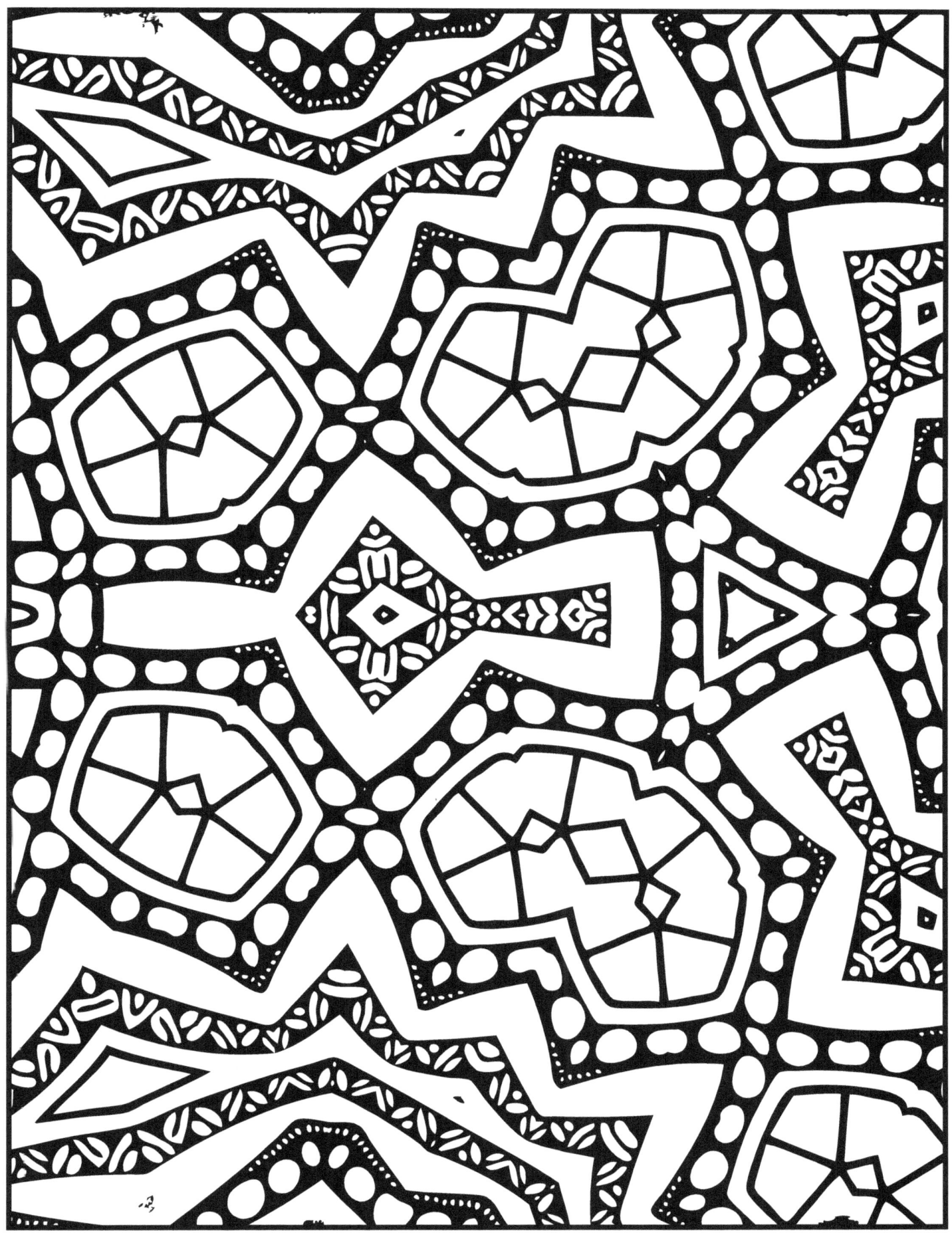

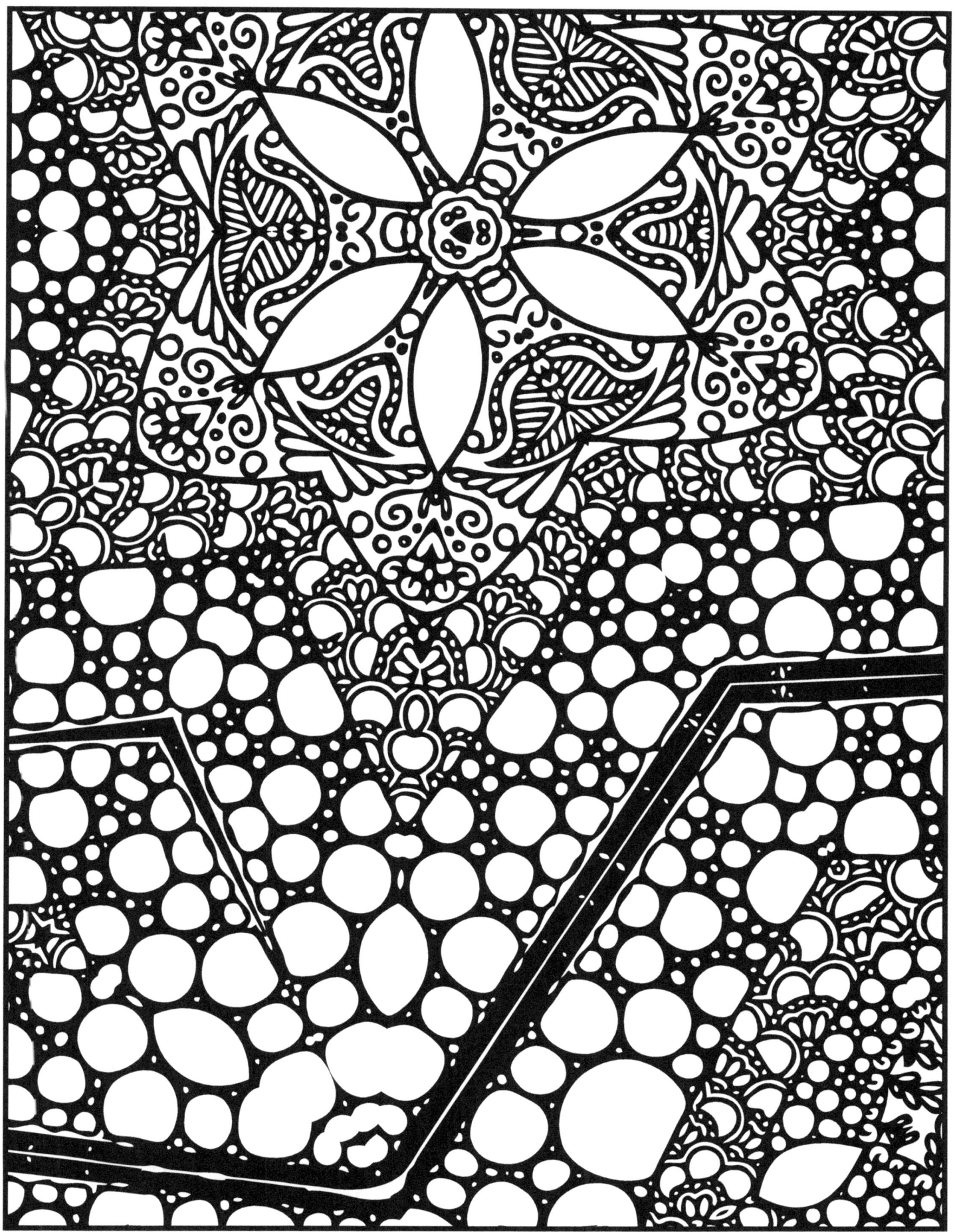

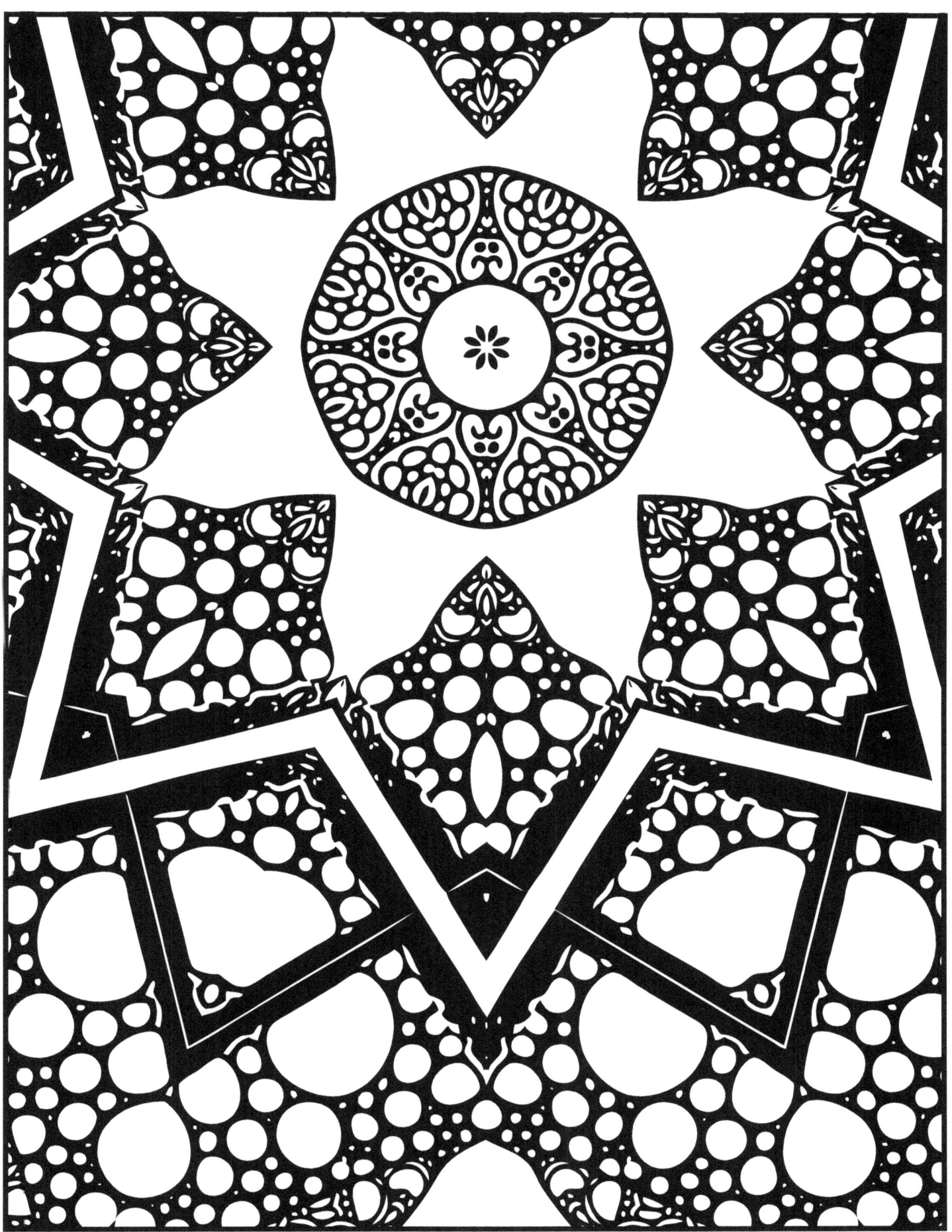

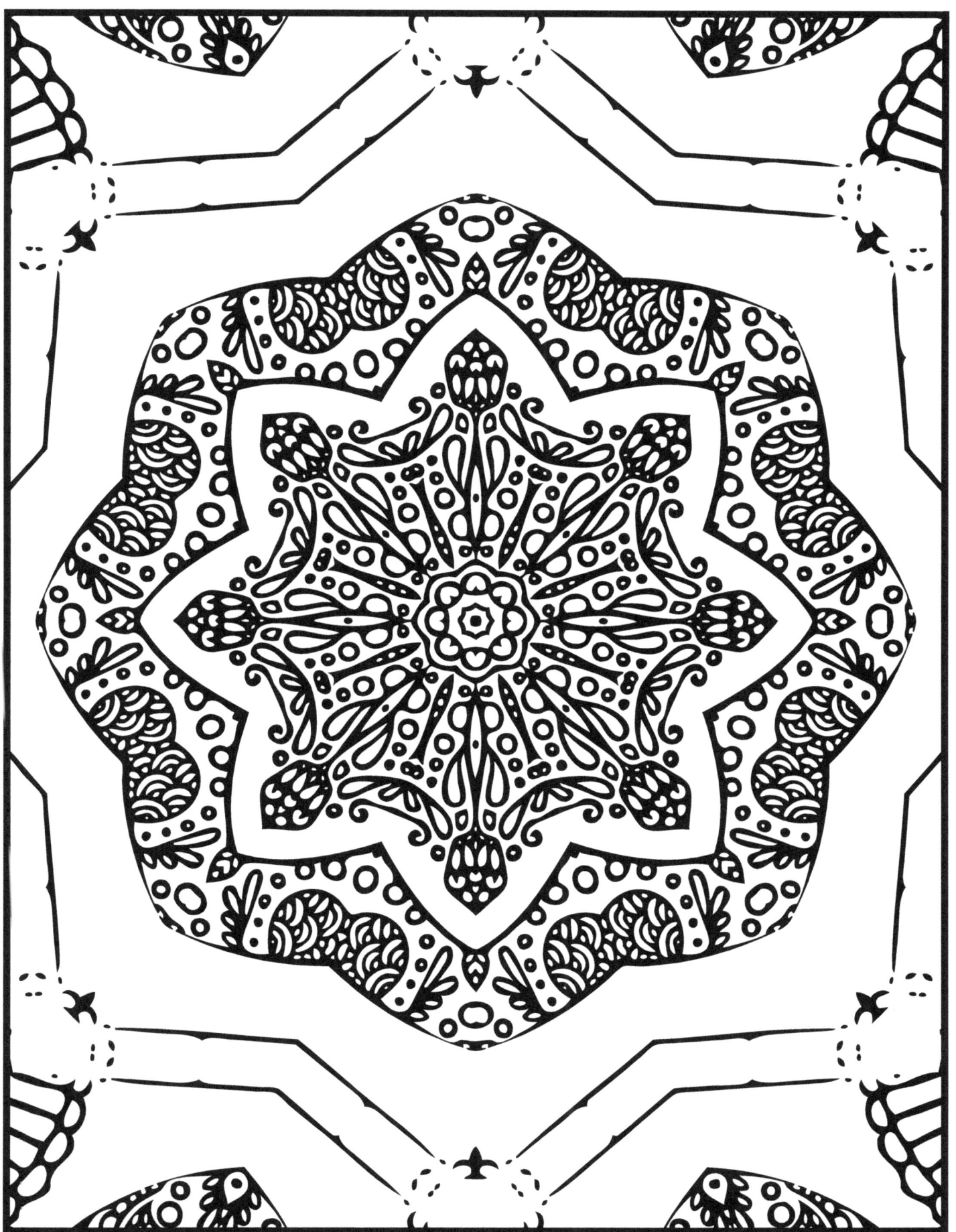

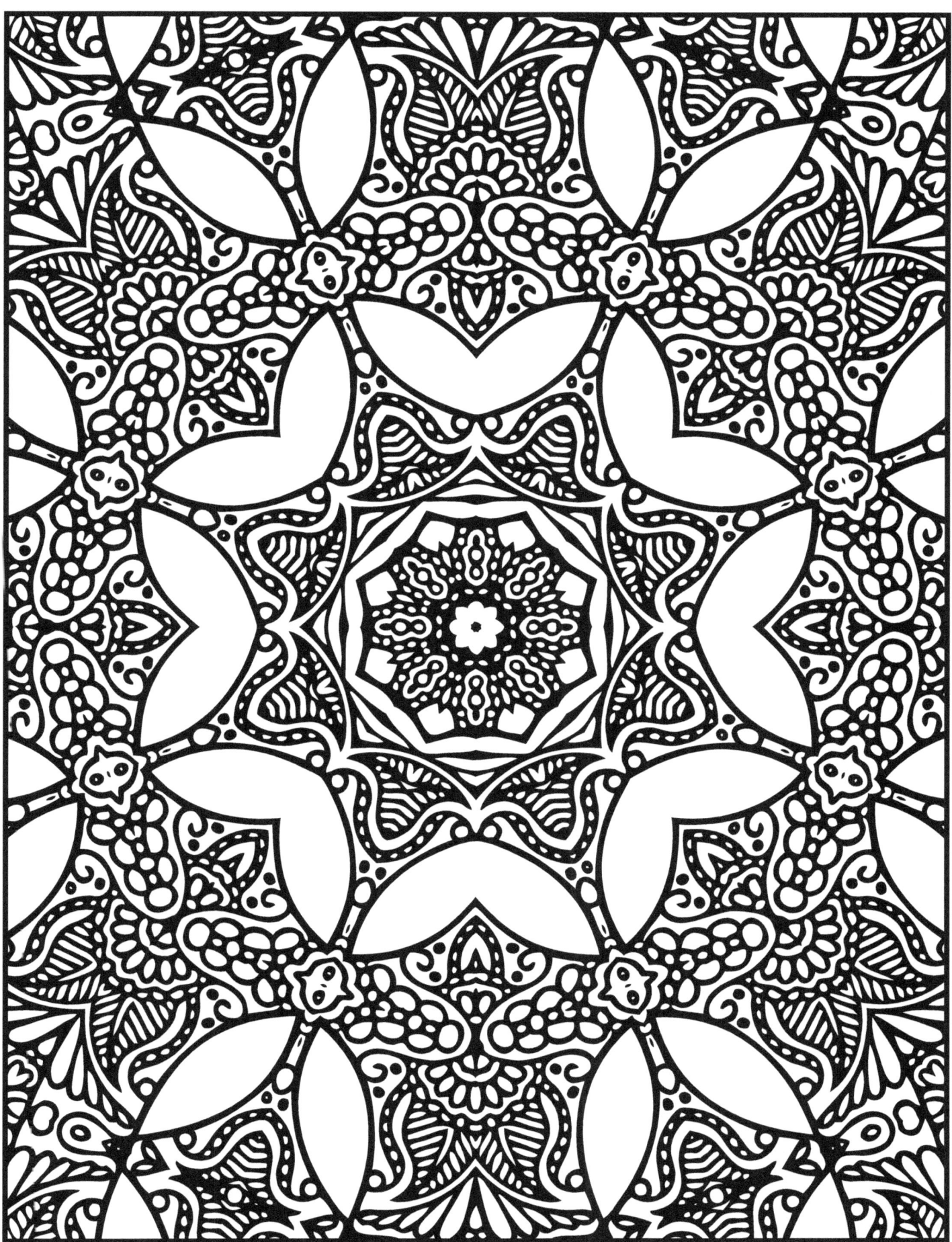

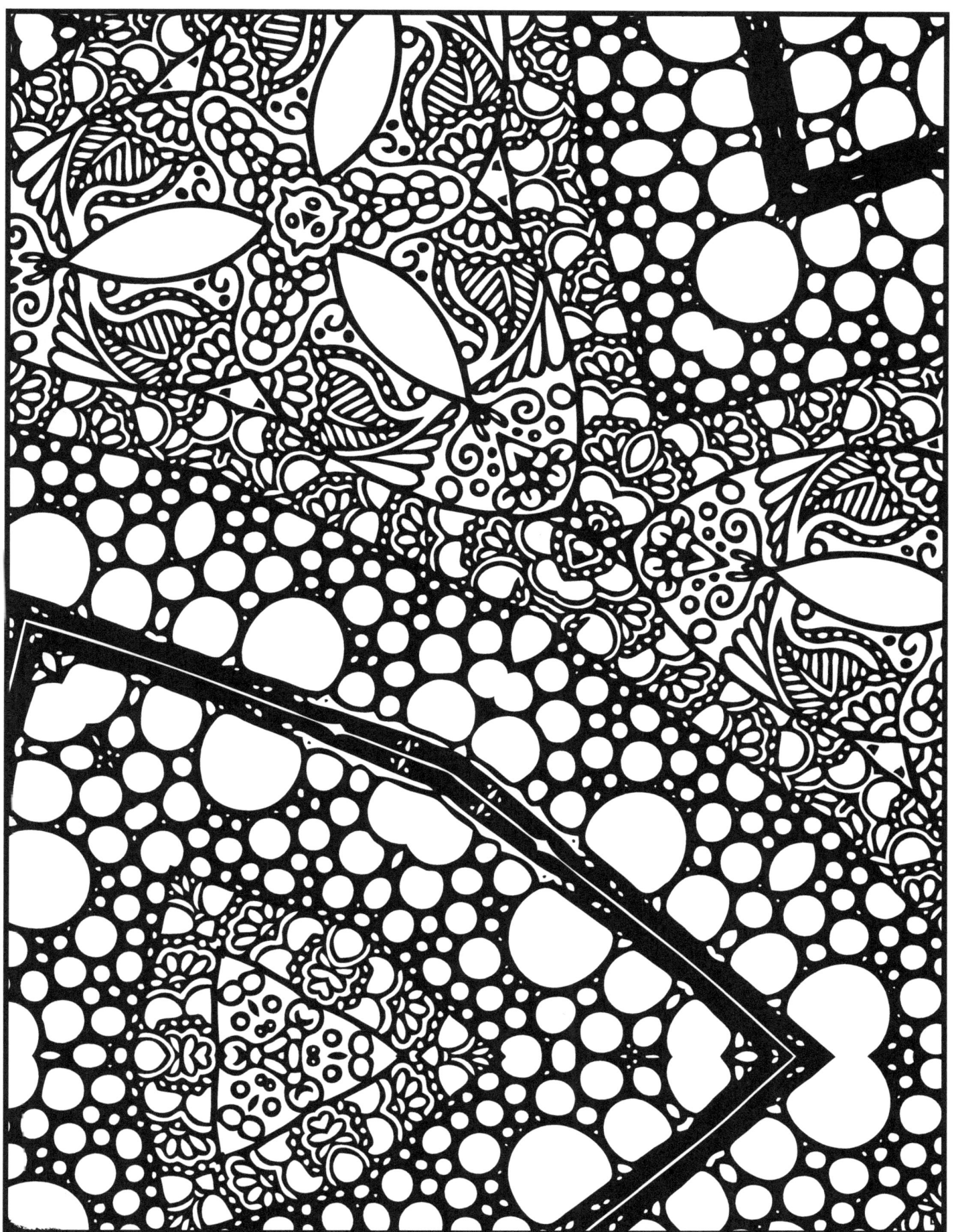

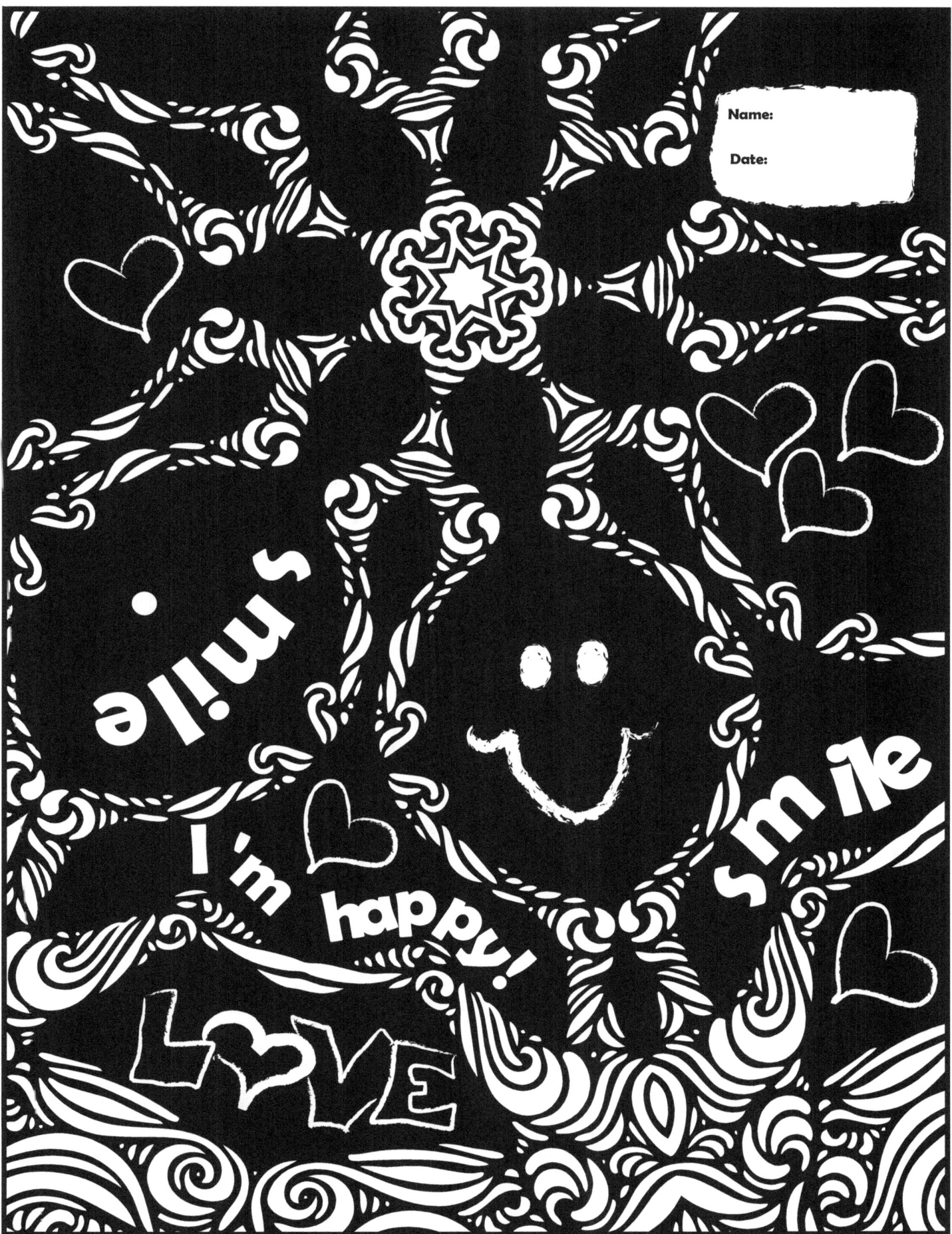

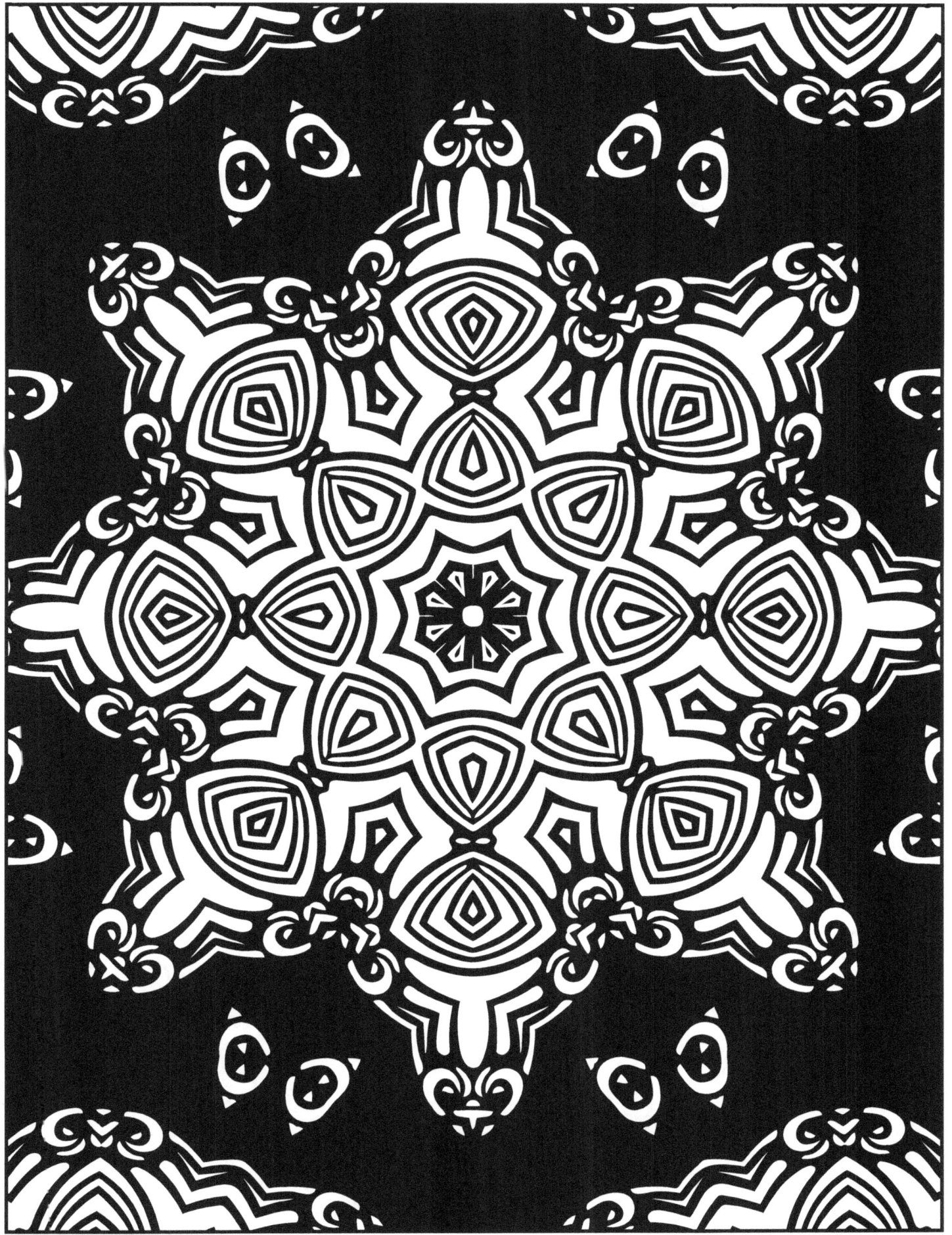

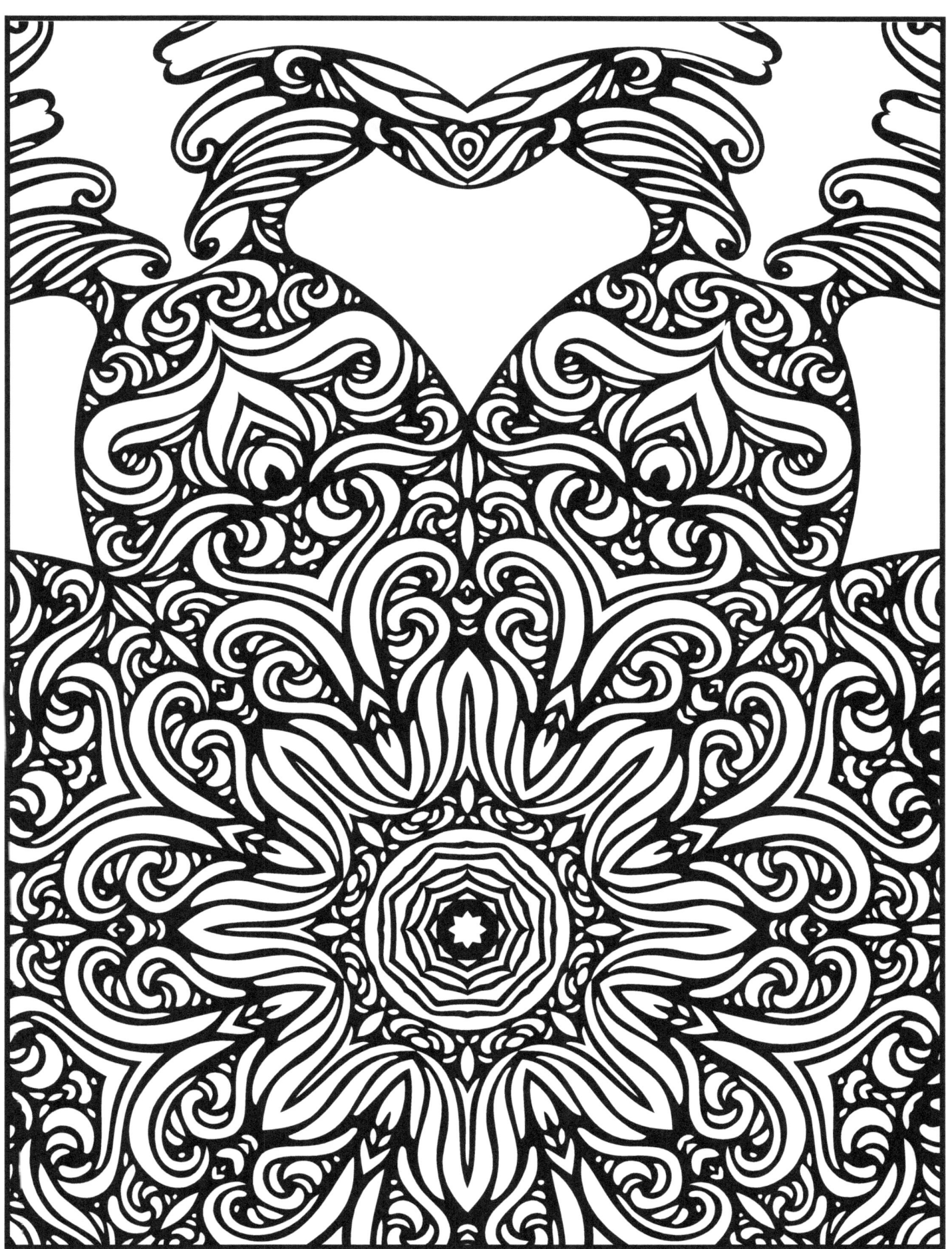

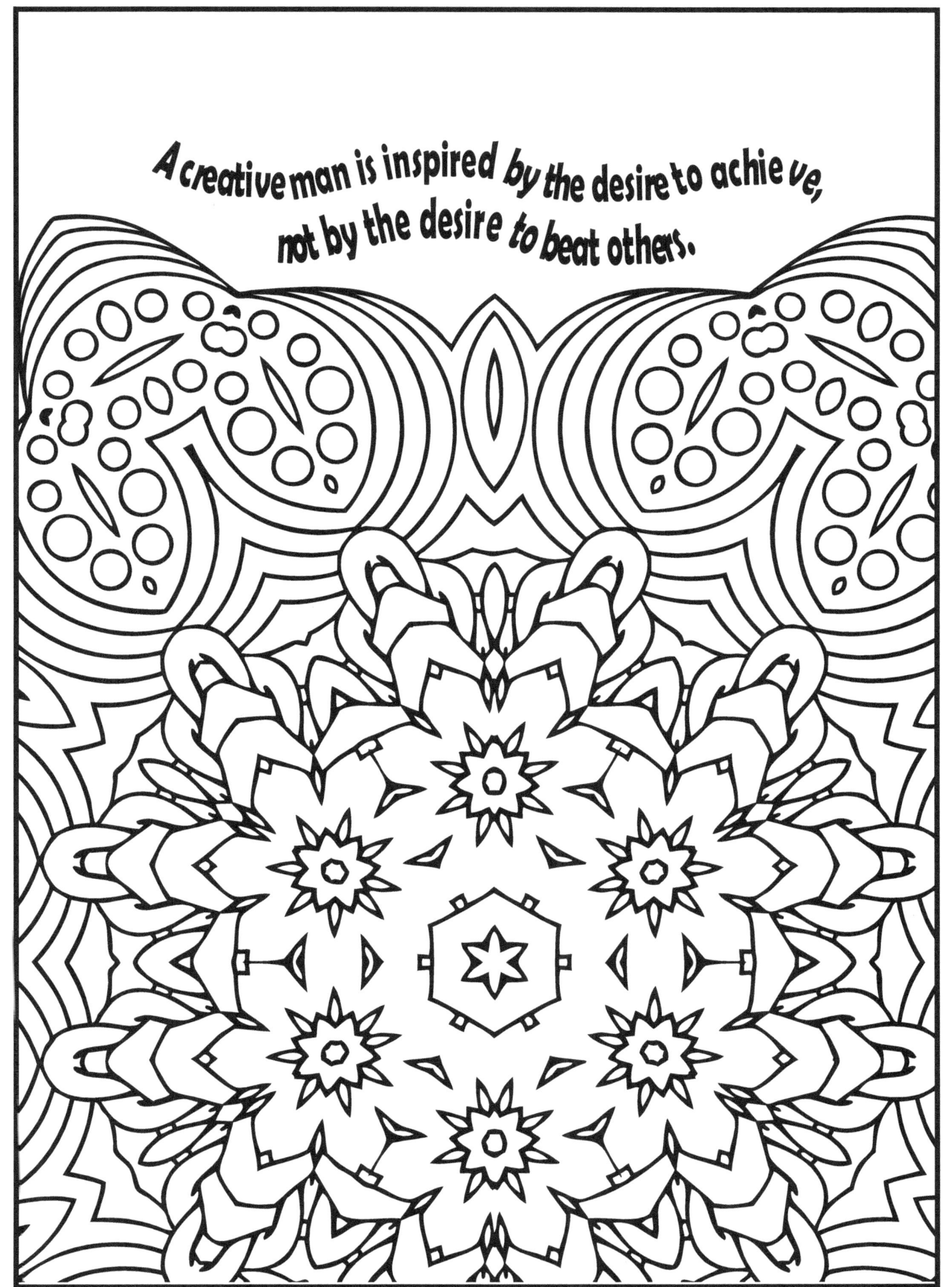

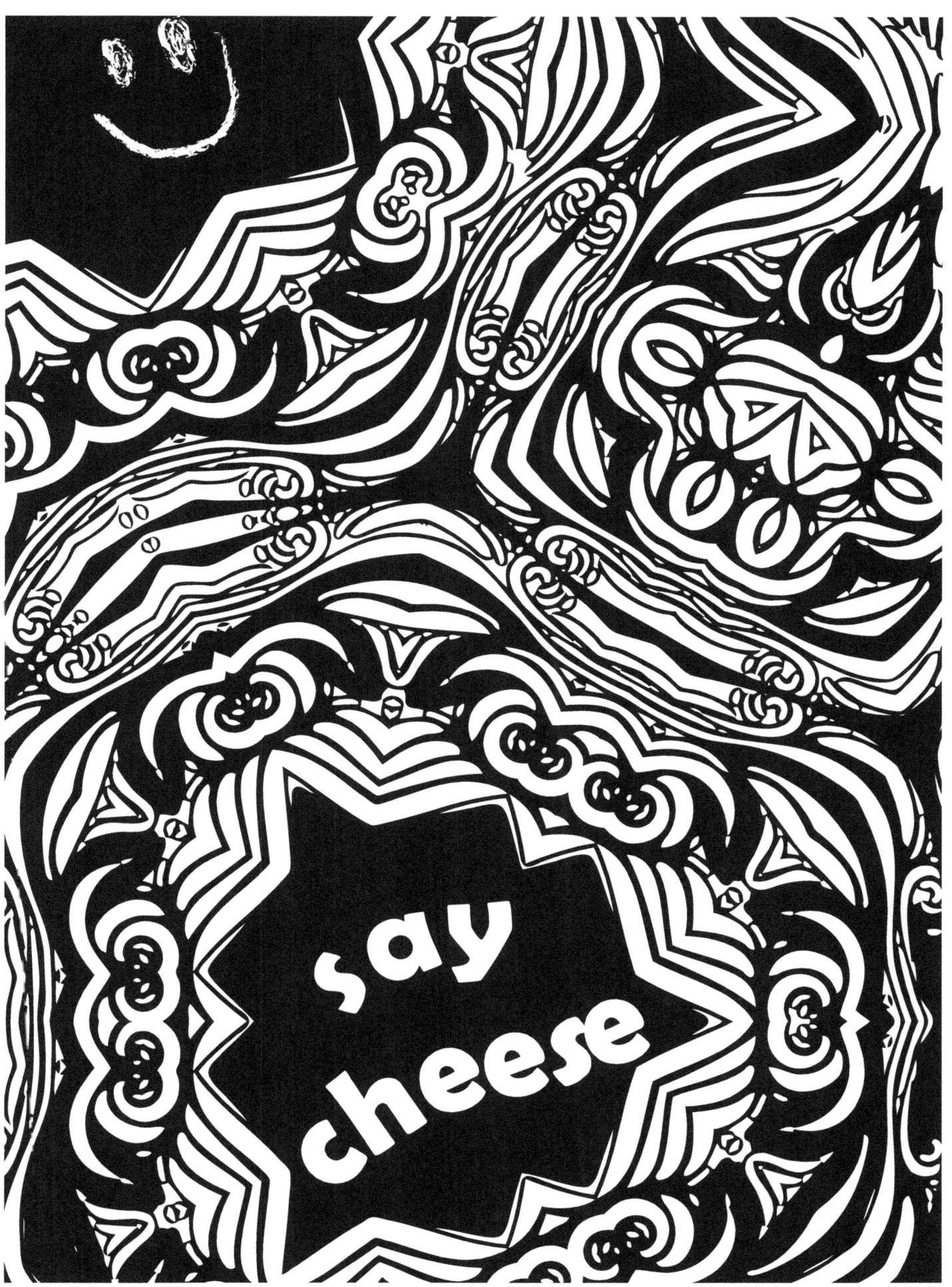

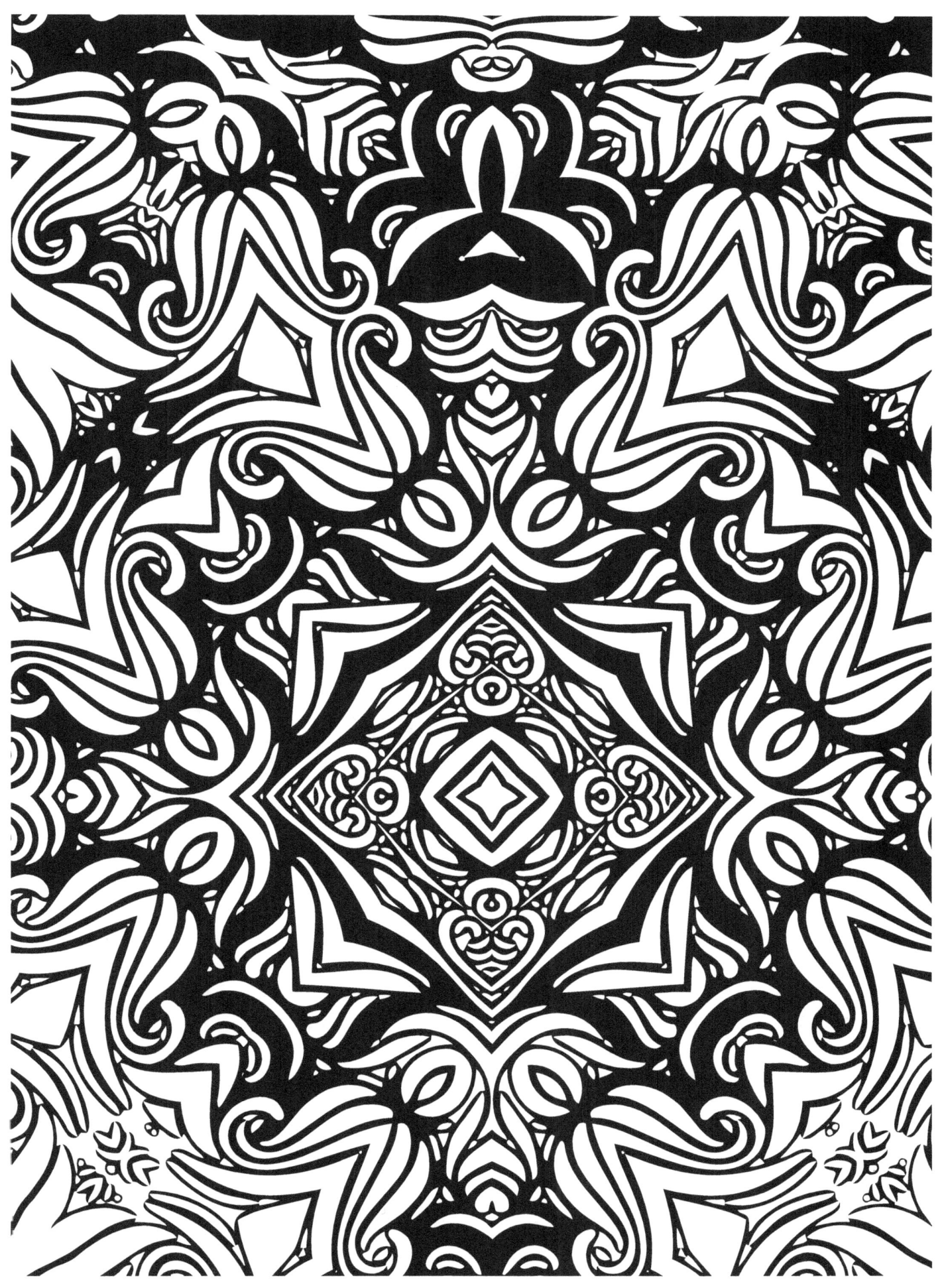

More From Andrea

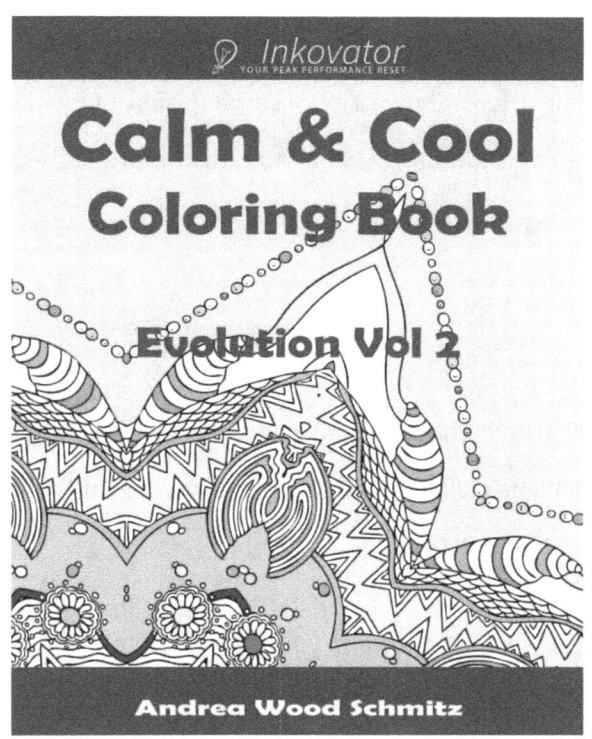

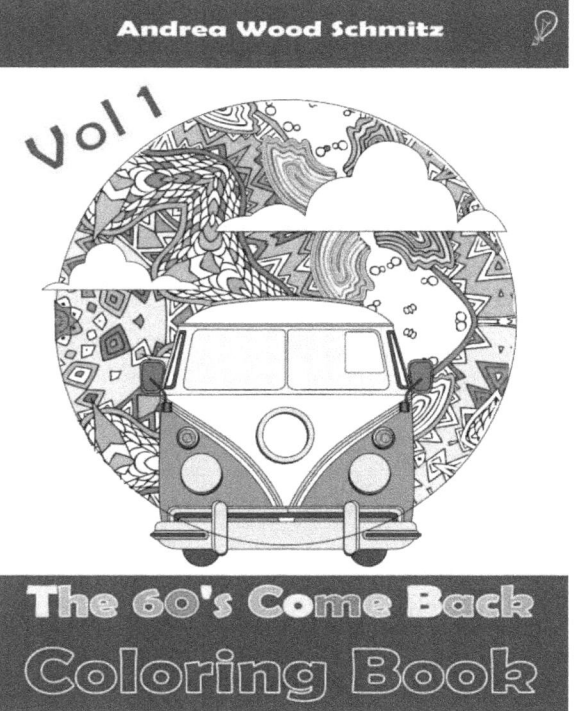

The Evolution continues with Calm & Cool, Vol 2. More whimsical, off-centered mandalas, some simple, some not, to calm you down or cool you off. Get it here: http://inkov.at/evolutionvol2

And if you like those, you'll absolutely enjoy the themed coloring books, here The 60's Come Back is filled with iconic memories of an era electric with energy, peace and love. Get it here: http://inkov.at/60vol1

For free samples from both books as well as updates for new publications, sign up at http://inkov.at/newsletter.

How else to connect with Andrea, chief Inkovator?

Follow her on Instagram: http://inkov.at/instagram

Become a fan on Facebook: http://inkov.at/facebook

Catch the growing collection of how-to-videos on Pinterest: http://inkov.at/pinterest

She's still trying to get the hang of Twitter over here: http://inkov.at/twitter

YouTube? If she starts up, then over here: http://inkov.at/youtube

Amazon author page, where you can see all books over here: http://inkov.at/amazon

Once a week I love to show off my fan's coloring. Here's how to get a social shout out by me.

First, color in a page and take a photo of it or of you coloring. Upload to one or more of the following platforms:

- Instagram
- Facebook
- Pinterest
- Twitter

Second, in your main post, where the image is, use the hashtag #inkovator so I can find it.

Third, keep your eyes peeled and every Friday I'll be giving be picking the #inkovator of the week and spreading some good cheer.

And finally, there is a private, privileged Club run by Inkovator and you are invited to join.

Join the Coloring Club run by Inkovators here: http://inkov.at/club

In the club, for a fraction of the cost of buying the books, you get access to 20 new coloring pages a month that you can download and print off as often as you want for personal coloring.

I know with 6 kids in my own house how much these get gobbled up as I've often wanted to have even my OWN copy multiple times.

Go Down In Amazon Review History

I LOVE an honest reviewer, don't you? Especially when they answer the questions I have in my mind...

That's why I want to commend you for stepping forward for the task at hand.

Now that you have your copy of Dream & Desire, Evolution Vol. 3 in your hands, won't you consider writing a review for others looking for a coloring book to purchase?

Start by having a look at the rich cover, noticing the brilliant colors. See how the design pops, how it's not symmetrical yet playful and inviting.

Turn the book over and read the back-cover, allowing the words to sink in deep. Coloring books are not known to be text heavy, but a good one will arouse your emotion and prepare you to enter into a creative energy as you start your coloring journey.

Now turn your eyes to the details within your book: Notice the attention to detail, the Color Test page, and the designs on the pages that follow. Imagine your favorite colors blending with the images, calling your creative energy to life.

What is your tool of choice? Markers? Freshly sharpened coloring pencils? How about crayons? Can you smell them?

Do you color alone? Do you sit with your children, spouse or parents to color? What is the atmosphere like? Peaceful? Crazy? Fun? Or simply precious, quiet fellowship with a special someone?

These are the impressions I'd love to hear about and that would make your review a true benefit to those who are looking for their next coloring adventure.

Please send your review to andrea@inkovator.com or consider placing your review on amazon at http://inkov.at/amazon.

I want to thank you for ordering this special edition of the Dream & Desire, Evolution Vol. 3 Adult Coloring book.

Andrea Wood Schmitz

Germany